On Life, Death And Nude Painting

Studio and other- world musings

Bernard Aimé Poulin

A Classic Perceptions Publication

For Michael,

I've written this book of reflections to encourage "thinking". How ironic that I would give a copy of reflections, words + reflections to someone whose thoughts, I have always admired.

Like a work of art you are a precious rarity. Michael Athens.

Marie + I have always known that.

Affectionately

Bernard

09/08/15

A Classic Perceptions Publication

Acknowledgements

Once again, without Marie at my side most of the ideas, comments and observations in this book would still be squirrelled away in drawers, cardboard boxes and computer files; gathering both physical and digital dust. Thank you love of my life for your unflagging encouragement, creativity and uncompromising ethics. Those who know you know well of what you are made. Those who don't are missing out on the best this world has to offer.

To my brother Claude, thank you for reassuring me that this compilation of often controversial ideas is more than gobbledygook. An incredible teacher and friend, your wisdom and professionalism are inspiring - possibly because almost everything you think, say and do is coated with a most ridiculously profound sense of humour - something of which this world needs more. The comedic stage is not the best it can be without your wit, sir. (Hint!)

And finally, to all of you I have encountered, stared at, wondered about and observed in parks, on the streets and in restaurants over the years. Thank you. I was the oddball leaning against a tree or a wall with a questioning look on his face, feverishly taking notes or sketching. Thanks for not thinking me a weirdo. But if you did, thanks for not calling the police. . .

I would also like to acknowledge the children of the world who constantly remind me that, at one time, we adults were all at our best as human beings - and could still be if we would simply try.

To the memory of my father Joseph Aimé Poulin (1914 - 1993)

In literature fathers are often presented as one of 2 categories - either the worst influential characters in the lives of a child or a wondrously impossible fabrication of heroic proportions. Mine was neither. He was human and therefore both strong and fragile.

Deep down inside I know that I must never grow into the sadness to which my beloved father eventually relegated himself. He was a man who's quiet strengths as a child I admired, whose determination and caring was unbounded, whose teaching abilities were immeasurable and whose humour was always brat-boyish. Nonetheless, his efforts were seemingly always being thwarted. And so his voice, once he no longer felt useful, became sullen and eventually front-porch-sit silent.

I cried the loss of my father during those years, the loss of a man I had long known but no longer knew. I cried because over time he dismissed himself to the halls of ennui and a self-imposed status of the to be forgotten.

During my growing years I was privy to the greater man that he was; privy to that very special patience he exercised, trying to pass down the strengths he so wished I would have - me, that eldest son for whom he felt he had done so little.

And so. . . this book of thoughts, wonderings, "questionings" and, yes, anger is dedicated to a man of overwhelming promise who died from being stifled - but not until he saw me secure, arrogantly striving and most especially "thinking" - that "thing" which he taught me was the most precious of human gifts - and the very one which should never be taken for granted. . . nor taken away.

Cher Papa, sitting amongst the angels suits you well. The talk and laugh fests must be incredible. Thank you for giving me more than you could ever know.

The Canadian sculptor, and stained glass artist Eleanor Milne was a self-assured preschooler the day she explained the drawing process to her mother : "First, I think and then I draw my think".

What a wondrously innocent way of describing the ability to first see and analyse with our mind. This small child wisely referred to the mind-sketch phase which always precedes the implementation of a "think" into a full fledged concrete rendering.

In her simple words, Milne described the very fabric of individual thought and creativity. Though visual artists spend many hours creating artworks, little of that rendering time is taken up thinking about what we are doing. Why? Because it has already been thought through prior to putting implements to surface. The actual act of rendering is next. This stage of the game demands we "feel" the "think" rather than logically review it. Why? Because the visual "logicality" of thinking has already been exercised and internalized. To create, to render a thought tangible, "feeling" must now become the main element and implement of "doing". Sensing a "think" is what gives it a life of its own. In essence, artwork creation is a balance between the perceptions of the mind's eye and the eventual "feelings" expressed through and for the senses.

Thinking a think is when we discuss with ourselves what it is we are wishing to say. Through a verbal or sketched out idea we then produce that thought visually. Drawing our think is the final act in making a consideration tangible - and ultimately "sharable".

On Life, Death And Nude Painting is a "think" sketch book. As Milne describes the process, I've thought my thoughts through and put them down. But here is where our goals differ. My collection of thinks are purposefully intermediary - incomplete. They are like thumbnail sketches - not finished drawings. They are "what do you think" thinks - not "here's what you should think" thinks. They are "reminders" to not forget to think and rethink what has been initially put forward. They are considerations only - thoughts wanting to be viewed and reviewed, again and again, and argued and discussed fully before "feeling" or considering themselves complete.

And so, in this book I share my "think" thumbnail sketches as they have emerged from the very base of my being over these past many years. All are "unvarnished" - i.e. : focussed on creating or "causing" conversations and discussions - whether heated or civil - as long as thinking occurs. Otherwise, left unshared they would have no other value than as invisible mental musings.

But still. . . Why a book of categorized random thoughts?

As individual thinkers we have a distinct advantage over those creatures who do not. Because we think, we can ordain the evolution and outcome of our being and our doings. Through thinking we can outline and determine the roads most or least travelled. We can define how we interpret that which came before, that which is now and how we will reach our tomorrows. When we freely exercise the power of thinking, we allow ourselves the possibility of linking our logical "thinks" with our intangibles - the wishes, dreams and feelings which lead us to futures befitting our "thought out" desires.

To think our thinks makes us not only individually powerful, it makes us strong members of a collective. It makes us valuable to our communities and, as such, individually and collectively worthy of the breaths we breathe.

That being said. Over the years I have seen both the collective and individual capacity to wonder, consider, argue and think weaken. Despite "thinking our think" being the most precious gift we have as free human beings, I'm worried. . .

As evolved as we seem to consider ourselves to be, the very idea of thinking our own thoughts is fighting a losing battle. Against what? Apathy? Being too comfortable to care? Having too many electronic gadgets rendering our thinks mindless? Or is it that we are beginning to slip quite comfortably into allowing others to do so for us? Almost imperceptibly, governments, corporations, advertising, insurance conglomerates, pharmaceutical enterprises, bureaucrats and a varied array of specialists are increasingly "thinking our thinks". This contributes to our being less and less creative and even less human than we have ever been since the beginning of time.

How are we ever to face the challenges of our individual and collective evolutions if we lose this capacity to study, to question, to share ideas, to discuss differences, to iron out, both honourably and diplomatically, the kinks in our national and international armours? Increasingly aggressive reaction, rather than thought out action, seems to be the only arrow in our quiver.

But then, we don't, either individually or collectively, seem to worry about that as much as we once did. Less and less seems to be "our problem". More and more, we relegate thinking about what ails the world to those who repeatedly "say" they know more than we do - yet do less and less than they promise they will.

But in the end, I just think. . . (no pun intended) that if I don't think, I'm either going to lose my ability to do so, or even before I do, someone will benevolently "demand" I should no longer bother. . . Just because it would be "best". . . or just. . . "the right thing to do". Why? Well, it seems "they" can do it more "efficiently" - more easily than I can.

If that were ever to be so, I would be sad. . . to never again be able to draw, or think another "think". . . And if that were so, I would become an embarrassment to those who love me, to my community and most especially to myself.

But all that being considered, I do acknowledge that taking on this book all at one go would be a heavy undertaking. Rather than get upset with me all at once, I suggest you spread it out over a reasonable period of time. But however you take it in, may your every "think", from wherever it comes, bring you feelings of being gloriously and powerfully alive - and most of all "truly" free to be the only you that can ever be.

Paul

To make the contents of the "Studio" section of this book more relevant to readers, I have chosen to outline the definitions of a few key words as they effect my daily foray into both the worlds of painting and writing.

Artwork

Artwork is any visual expression created by anybody - whether artist or not - whether child or adult. Artwork, as a concept, has a wide range of acceptability : from amateur scribble to work produced by the technically proficient and even that created by the somewhat talented. What separates artwork from "art" is that artwork speaks more to its creator's level of abilities than to an artwork's messaging strengths or stand alone connection with a viewer.

Though artwork may aspire to be art, it is not yet "there". For all intents and purposes, artwork creation is related more to rendering excellence than to "saying something".

Most of us who are creative in the visual arts are at an artwork creation level. This statement is not meant to belittle the "artwork" connection or effort. It simply indicates the levels at which most resulting creations and their creators function in this era of prolific artwork rendering.

And so, most of us creating in the visual arts field legitimately fit somewhere within the wide range of artwork-creator categories, such as : apprentice, amateur, talented painter, sculptor, carver, printer, photographer, sketcher, visual artist, etc. i.e. : those who honourably concentrate on "doing" artwork rather than those who need to be seen to be "artists".

The most proficient and talented amongst us (within this category) often legitimately become recognized and appreciated for the rendering excellence of the "artworks" we produce.

Visual Artist *(catch-all phrase)*

One who "does" or creates artwork.

Art

Art is artwork rising to a level of expression and communication which, as a statement, reaches above and beyond the norm in both technical and creative élan. Its capacity to reach out, to touch, to move, to awe and to speak to viewers surpasses anything the basic craft of or technical skill in artwork can conjure. At its highest level of expression, "art" becomes "masterpiece" and its creator a "master".

Art is born of one who has a unique ability to sense the powers, wonders and horrors of it all and is capable of transmitting those sentiments to the world beyond that artist's own visions and environs. Only an artist can be said to be the creator of "art" and only art can be said to have been created by an artist.

Artist

An artist is someone who creates artwork which rises to a level worthy of the titles art and/or masterwork. In essence, the message, shared idea or emotion of such an artwork created surpasses by much the basic physicality of the paint and canvas, stone, marble, photo rendition or 3-D existence used to physically render that piece.

The same criteria apply to any other field of creativity. For example: a piano player is a hobbyist. A student of the piano, an apprentice. A pianist is a trained technician good enough to amuse and even mesmerize an audience with borrowed imagery. An artist of the instrument is a professional who not only dazzles with imagery in a most sensual way - he or she gives life to sounds beyond a physical execution or representation of them - and probably can do so even if the instrument being played has only three working keys.

Master - Masterpiece

Though today we often too casually define much of what is ordinary as incredible and (worse) "awesome", a masterpiece is more realistically the only creation with which such accolades can justifiably be associated.

The creation of an Art statement is a search for excellence by someone who, despite his or her human limitations, rises somehow high above the norm in the expression of a thought, feeling, idea or concept.

A masterpiece is more often than not the apex of such a search - the ultimate in expression - the most grandiose of thoughts conveyed - even amongst many other artworks which can also legitimately take on the title of "art".

A masterpiece is always the result of an artistic effort gone "viral", gone superior and extraordinary despite the limitations of an individual's imaginings. A masterpiece is an artistic rendering magically imbued with an inspired meaning or enigma which can only universally awe the world.

And yet, at the same time, Art and Masterpieces are never referred to or associated with perfection. Perfection implies : impossible to replicate or best i.e. : "nothing more or better can be achieved".

In art there is no "end", no completeness or total achievement. There is always room to reach beyond the unreachable. And this is why Art relates to an ongoing search for the best we can be, the greatness that can always be achieved and this, despite what has been done before. Art is about the fluidity of excellence, never the rigidity of perfection.

Naturally, an artist and/or a master artist being so gifted, and the work created so incredible, the resulting impact of both are often erroneously referred to as perfection. But then, creative expression at a level that is uncommon often elicits negative rather than positive responses at the time of their rendering.

Nonetheless, masterworks always defy normality, speak to excellence and in so doing reject commonality and the very idea of its equal and opposite : perfection.

For all intents and purposes, the best in art, invention, creativity, composition, writing, etc. is what defines the never-ending greatness that we humans are capable of striving for and achieving.

Masterworks convince us that humanity's destiny should never be under-estimated or belittled by our incessant collective need to afford recognition, acceptable functioning level status and adulation to that which is easy or lowest common denominator.

On Life, Death And Nude Painting

Studio and other- world musings

A Classic Perceptions Publication

Contents of Studio Musings

On Art

Artwork is not necessarily art. But art is necessarily artwork. - 2014 *

To become art - to evolve to a level of reaching out, of sharing, of message - artwork must be more than an ego massage. - 2014 *

If our artwork has nothing to say to us, it will have even less to say to others. - 2013 *

It's not that a troubled soul cannot create artwork. It can. But for the resulting work to be "art", it must stretch beyond being a therapeutic exercise. - i.e. : it must rise to a connectedness with the soul's of others.

Munch's work is a prime example. The angst represented isn't simply his. It has a universal quality to it. The world identifies with his interpretations of pain, sorrow, anxiety, worry, sadness and exaltation. Everyone recognizes through his eyes what they themselves experience. That it is not simply a mirrored reflection of his life; that it is universal in scope is what makes Munch's work "art". – 2013 *

Cartoons, comic strips (call them what you will) are the most direct, the most powerfully "connecting" visual art forms of the 21st century - followed closely by advertising. Ironically, the former keep us sane while the latter "consumes" us. - 2013 *

Anyone can paint, draw, sculpt or write poetry. The question is not how well we explain what we have painted or written but how well the work speaks for itself.- 2009 *

Artwork should always say more than the title representing it. - 2009 *

When a visual artist does not pompously promote the visionary relevance of his or her work, that artwork has a chance to communicate on its own what it has been created to say. - 2007 *

When I wash brushes in the clean-up area of my studio, no one disturbs me "working". But when I return to the easel to paint, most people feel comfortable enough to disrupt this activity. Often times, the worst perpetrators are painters themselves. How respectful we are of someone's creative efforts is sometimes more telling than how we perceive them or the end product.- 2007 *

*Lorsqu'on se sent obligé de constamment répéter qu'une oeuvre "vient nous chercher" est-ce que c'est pour cacher le fait qu'elle n'a, en vérité, aucune capacité de le faire? - 2006 **

Artwork, when it is Art, tells a story. It relates. It reaches out and touches. It moves and enters a receiving soul. And the greater the artwork, the greater its capacity to communicate time, place and events which are beyond the artist's private space. And when that happens, art IS. - 2006 *

Art is about the concept, the statement, the subject. Artwork about the creator. - 2005 *

The very idea of "seeing into the depths of an artist's suffering" is to play at being a psychiatrist or psychologist - and a bad one at that. This concept has been routinely over-rated and bizarre - witness the attitudes we display concerning the likes of Van Gogh, Gauguin and Caravaggio.
To muse on the sufferings of another is to find a rather unsavoury pleasure in an individual's purported art-therapy sessions - and not the content of his or her artwork or "art". . . . - 2005 *

Art is born of those who sense the powers and wonders and horrors of it all and are capable of transmitting those sentiments to viewers - as these relate to them also. - 2005 *

In the arts, validity and vapidity are more closely related than we would imagine. Without a process imbued with the former, the end result is often nothing more than the latter. - 2004 *

The arts are a counter-balance to the demands of conformity, to a submission to the status quo and to lowest common denominator expectations concocted by an environment become complacent. - 2003 *

There appears to be a lot of interest in playing with paint, textures, materials; discovering what happens when they are all thrown together - a bit like tossing scrabble squares into the air; waiting to see what that might cause them to spell.

Possibly then, my work is more obsession than passion. . . I oddly am focussed on getting the "spelling" right in the hope viewers get the message. - 2002 *

There is so much talk about art and yet, so little of it getting done. - 2002 *

Contemporary artwork has more to do with the "product" of an artistic statement than the content of it. - 2002 *

Whether figurative, non-representational or abstract, contemporary artwork too often fails to communicate anything more vital than itself - and that is never enough to sustain even a modicum of recognition or longevity. - 2001 *

Some of the most moving pictures are stills - 2000 *

When excellent, artwork is a question not an answer - 2000 *

Fine art is about the world beyond the artist, art therapy about the producer of the artwork - 2000 *

As there are any number of inane conversations, there are also many elaborate and technically complex issues to be discussed. As there are many terse expletives, there are also fluid and effusive eulogies. And as there are more thick novels, obese with dreg than

1.4

there are thin recollections of "Petit Prince" excellence, it should be no surprise that so many more navel-gazing images exist in galleries than powerful, soothing or deliciously rich masterpieces. - 1999 *

The contemporary visual arts world is like Hollywood, far too much about the actors and not the acting; too much about being than doing, too much about entertaining than moving or being moved. - 1998 *

Art is never abstract and always is... - 1997 *

Art emerges when technical prowess, deftly realised, frees us to completely immerse our "self" into the fluidity of the task at hand. - 1997 *

Contemporary artwork is much more a pessimistic, self-centred expression of primal fear, (the anxiety of not being recognized and accepted as "one of the clan"), than an optimistic and comfortable need to express unique personal observations. As such, it is a reflection of the environment from which it stems. - 1997 *

Art is our maker, never our slave. - 1997 *

Art is the most potent measure of the heartbeat of a nation, the colour of its imagination and the intensity of a country's commitment to the well-being of its citizens. - 1997 *

Either the work speaks for itself or it shouldn't be. - 1995 *

1.5

Art cannot and does not survive in an experiential and/or emotional vacuum. - 1993 *

There is very little proof that the major portion of that which is perceived to be "contemporary art"; (i.e.: art which communicates an expression of our times), is in fact artful in the traditional sense. Much of it, these past fifty years, has never been more than a tool to shock, to push away - lacking, as it often does, the capacity to legitimately reach out and deeply move. And yet, it does speak volumes as to the context from which it springs.

To touch is now perceived as aberrant, perverse, abusive and degrading. Modern contact is relegated to pushing, confronting, slapping, "high-fiving", fist bumping. These have replaced holding, hugging, touching and stroking.

Avoidance of sensuality through sharp and quick "grab and run" contacts, replacing lingering communion and connection, is more the norm than a rarity today.

The neuroses of warrior-like compensation have replaced the satisfaction of selfless giving and delicious receiving as even foreplay becomes excessive, in light of what is truly erotic and pleasurable. Oddly, erotica is now more akin to what is pornographic than to what is sensual. But if this is what the artwork of our times is reflecting, then possibly, as we look around us. . . it is legitimate. - 1990 *

Contemporary artworks often resemble television ads bolstered by an attention grabbing volume boost. The annoyance generated by the strident imposition of themselves immediately negates the existence of any worthy message they may try to convey. - 1990 *

Too often we scoff at those who do not "understand" our artwork whilst revelling in the arrogant belief that this legitimizes our dabblings. - 1990 *

If it were not for Art, community living would quickly become unbearable. - 1987 *

Erroneously, the appropriation of the title artist presumes (or imposes upon others) that the work produced is "art". - 1984 *

*Art is the telling of stories. - (Neil Peart) - *

Art is the result of passionately sharing the generous ravings which emanate from the depths of the hearts and souls of those rare individuals called artists. - 1981 *

How ironic it is that those who often fail at "doing" artwork become the art-bureaucrats who judge and acquire for public spaces the work of those who successfully "do" - 1980 *

Good artwork does not focus on being beautiful but rather on being beautifully rendered. - 1978 *

If an irritated 11 month old, spreading feces on the walls of his room, is not considered an expressionist, how is it that any 20, 30 or 50 year old painter, spreading "angst" or their superior "visions" on canvas, can be entitled so? - 1976 *

Consumers buy artwork to fit their pocketbook and their living room's colour scheme, collectors the colour scheme of their

1.7

imagination.

Consumers buy our work if it makes them feel comfortable, collectors if the work says something they would never have thought possible.

Consumers buy artwork if the visual artist sees the same things they do. Collectors, because familiar things are rendered differently. - *

We are too much into being artists and not enough into doing artwork. The whole process has been bastardized - now being more about recognition than about artwork creation. - *

Artwork is about how well we speak, Art about the content of our statement. - *

Art is what stops the structured order of civilization from becoming oppressive. - *

Art exists when the passionate statement of an individual is expressed via an inanimate object whose inert physicality is transcended - becoming a statement, a connection with others; in essence, something more than itself or its "artist". When less than this, it is artwork. When less than that – basic self-expression. When extraordinary, it is a masterpiece. - *

Art happens when the eye is objective and the hand is free to play. - *

*It's not that people can't recognize art, but that they are not even looking for it. - (Louis Dudek) **

As old pieces of furniture are not necessarily antiques, old paintings are not necessarily masterpieces. - *

When the time comes and there is no art, we will be no more. - *

Contemporary advertising has filled the void created by the visual art world's stand against every man. - *

*Lorsque les Barbies anorexiques représentent l'esthétique nouvelle, le statut de victime que cet état physique représente ne peut faire autrement que d'être le nouvel héroïsme qu'on vend à nos enfants - et par ce fait, les arts ne font qu'exprimer la situation dépressive qui parfois envahi le présent don't font face ces mêmes enfants. - *

When art exists despite its tormentors, it is worthy art indeed. - *

Art in all its myriad forms is not a therapeutic process yet it is the only form of communication which digs deep enough that an appreciation of it prevents individual and societal decay. - *

Nothing which mars or destroys the integrity of creation is art. Graffiti imposed is nothing but vandalism - destructive rather than creative; and in that light is not "art" nor even artwork. When a prima facie reason for existence is to spit upon someone else's creative effort or space, society has serious cause to look itself in the mirror when it bows to such anarchy. - *

When I impose upon the world my artwork, there is very little life in it. But when I take notice of the world and its offerings - how it affects who I am and how I feel about this environment of discoveries, with its ever altered balance of pleasures and pain - my work is immediately more vibrant. - *

The quality, the essence of all Japanese art forms is measured first by the mastery of technical skill and secondly by the unique creative talent of a specific individual who has the ability to meld the two aspects into not only a coherent composition but also a level of mesmerizing poetry.
In essence, the successful combination of these two elements transforms a wondrously well rendered artwork into the mystery that is "Art". - *

Artwork made easy may often be pretty but it is never art. - *

Having a style of one's own must not be confused with being consistent in the repetition of drawing and painting errors. - *

Art has never been, nor will it ever be, a revered object - even less a mundane ordinary object. Art is a spiritual and sensual presence, not a physical one. - *

When the passionate mind and soul of one human being shares the best of itself with another, an awe inspiring compact occurs. This is when we know we are in the presence of more than standard artwork, more than an ordinary creator. - *

Artistic expression allows those who feel imposed upon by the more rigid edges of society to speak freely and without guilt. - *

Artwork is self-expression which makes creators feel like artists; whether they are or are not. Art is a message which so moves and touches multitudes, the title of artist is soon bestowed upon its creator. - *

If the limited definition of what is "contemporary art" is the only voice we have, one day we will be forced to recognize that we've been "muted" by our own remote. - *

For art to be truly art it needs return to its communicable essence, the premise that the manner in which it is expressed is unique and yet intensely relevant to more than its creator. - *

Too often, the value of artwork is measured by who owns or trades it but rarely by who appreciates it. - *

Returning art to the people is the first step in eliminating the need to "bring art to the people". - *

Culture is not an expense. . . It is an investment. - *

Once the equalizer, art has sadly come to be the very symbol of dividsion - separating those who are "in" from those who are not. - *

To our mothers the artwork we produce is always beautiful. That is why our mother's words are rarely critiques, our self-expressions rarely artwork and, even more rarely, art. - *

Artwork is not good or bad because someone says it is. Artwork is good or bad because it inevitably proves itself to be good or bad. - *

Art is born of the pigment of imagination. - *

Very often the sentiments, perceptions and feelings we use to verbally express ourselves are the same which destroy the impact of visual artworks. - *

The most contemporary of artistic mentors are more than willing to describe for us the essence of art. But by the time they reach that stage of being seen to be wise, we are often no longer amenable to being taught. - *

A person who loves visual representation but can't tell the difference between a reproduction and an original is akin to someone who prefers TV soccer to actually being there. - *

As in many other fields, depth in art can either be deeply profound or cavernously vapid. And as is often the case, time and the general public are inevitably the best arbiters. - *

The more realistically something is rendered, the more pastiche, made-up or academic it appears to be. The more impressionistically something is rendered, the more real it "feels". - *

Artwork which allows us to delve into it, to plumb its depths, to extricate its meanings, foibles and intricacies is more coherent, more calming and more powerful than any other. It goes to the need to connect which resides within us all. - *

A work of art must relate. It must be a part of, or emanate from and constantly strive to reach back to that world from which it stems. - *

Art is an ordinary thought expressed extraordinarily. - *

When applying contemporary standards to the past. . . we often invariably elevate the most mundane of pre-twentieth century artwork to the level of master work; not because the work is good but simply because it is old and because we naively believe that if it is old it is good. Crassly, we equate old with dead and that which is dead and old with marketability and in our silly way with "artistry". - *

Art as a tool of communication, a language of the essence of man, has never left us. We have left it. - *

The more we impose a meaning upon a subject the less meaning it conveys. - *

An artist of consequence is not one to pompously promote the visionary relevance of his or her work. And because he or she does not, the artwork has a chance to communicate on its own what it has been created to say. - *

It is not what we have to say about a subject but rather what a subject has to say about us that makes for good artwork. - *

My purpose in life is not to be seen to be a great creator of paintings but to create the best paintings I can in the hopes that surely. . . possibly, maybe, one day, one of these artworks will have the power to move, to touch the hearts and souls of many. - *

Art isn't - unless it takes us out of ourselves and away from self-indulgent babbling and whining. - *

The figurative well rendered is based on logical sensuality whereas the abstract is rooted in sensual logic. - *

When technique or style overshadows the statement of a painting, it is comparable to the paint job on a car outshining the performance. - *

We eventually grow into the artwork we make. It creates us. - *

The elements which make artwork excellent don`t change simply because the "isms, techniques or equipment do. - *

*Lorsqu'on s'attarde trop au style de l'expression, on finit par louanger et flatter sans capter rien du contenu. Mais je suis peut-être trop exigeant. Peut-être qu'il n'y a pas matière à comprendre. - ***

Art renews itself, changes, evolves, speaks out and is heard, despite our desperate efforts to sabotage it. - *

The most fundamental benefit of the arts is that they recognize each individual style within a necessarily homogenous environment. - *

A blob of red paint on its own is never more than its physical manifestation. It can never be anything more until it has been "contextualized" - fit into a venue of space and time, whereby it gains a foothold on relevance and tangibility. - *

Contemporary fiscal reality dictates that in difficult times government cuts must be made - whether local, provincial or federal. Such cuts occur first in those areas considered superfluous; unimportant in the grand scheme of things. And so, the first financial hits take place in the creative arena - the visual arts and music. And yet, when financial woes continue, the first peoples recruited, to fund-raise for in-need services, are those self-same rejected "artistic elements". - *

1.14

*(North) American culture is more adept at the arts that make life easier than in those that embellish it. - (Alexis de Tocqueville) ***

It is impossible to impose relevance upon the elements of an artistic expression. A rectangle can no more pretend at emotive and/or communicative powers than an ant will itself anteater. Yet, if that shape and its context are compatible and the expression is imbued with balance, discipline, integrity, wisdom and a willingness to communicate without artifice, the rectangle then easily becomes relevant in and of itself. - *

The essence of much of what is called "modern art" has deteriorated to such a level of irrelevance that all it can say is: "I am here, I am now and I will be heard!!! And if you don't understand the undisciplined, unstructured and unconstrained spits I throw at you, in between thumb-sucks. . . Then, Fuck you!" - *

Much of what is considered contemporary art can only be defined as the knack of making complex that which is simple. - *

Despite normal evolution, contemporary dance and musical composition retain natural movement and rhythm as foundational. On the other hand, our much too coddled and revered visual arts sadly suffer at their own hand - ignoring if not negating their base, their roots - this through a lack of respect for self, craft and communal relevance. - *

What contemporary Europe has in visual art is history, masterworks, and nostalgia, not better contemporary art. - *

Art is not, never has been and never will be an act, statement or symbol of imposition. Art is an invitation, a sharing. That we may be pleased or not by the offering is another matter altogether. - *

1.15

Art voices what is felt when we observe and are observed. It cannot be curbed by order or design, judgements, censure or morals. This is not to say that artists or the arts are or should be amoral or immoral but rather that the realm of the arts exists within a natural morality - despite the oppressions or obsessions of institutionalized corporate, governmental, religious or personal agendas. - *

Propaganda is never art, nor art propaganda. If anything, artworks of this ilk are nothing less than mind graffiti, imposed advertising, promotion and marketing of the worst kind by the least sensitive of ideologists - those who value no other thought or needs than their own. - *

During difficult periods, throughout the evolution of man, (plagues, war, famine), the arts have depicted both the decrepit and the grand nature of humanity - and in the end its ability to defeat, i.e. : surmount and move beyond the odds. By their very nature, the arts encourage survival instincts, the will to overcome despite all obstacles - natural and man-made. They celebrate and point out, state and question human foibles as well as excellence.
Without the arts, there is no celebration or castigation of man. And without them, no equilibrium in the representation of evolution, no future forecast, no objective truth. - *

Contemporary art too often focuses on the subjective interpretation of a subject - or not on the subject at all but rather on the feelings and intimations of a visual artist who's judgement and or perceptions may not necessarily be the definitive source for philosophic repartee on a specific topic. For creation by reaction demands much less in the area of awareness than does creation by objective analysis. - *

1.16

Figurative art encourages a return to naive reflection - basic contemplation on the root skills of humanity. It is comprehensible, non-threatening. It encourages individual wondering and perception in a world whose technological advances more than hint at a loss of autonomy and individual thought. - *

Some of the most repeated words in the traditional visual arts have been form, grace, rhythm, movement, power, emotion and mystery. In the late 19th century, the Impressionists imbued these basic elements with a new "élan"; filtering them through a lens of light and colour. Though rebellious in their quest, they nonetheless remained respectful; never disfiguring the main essence of each of the foundational compositional elements in the traditional visual arts. - *

Regardless of "ism" or awesomeness perceived to exist in contemporary artwork, the only quality worthy of note is that which raises the communication of content above and beyond the ordinary. Our ability to not only look but see, not only listen but hear, will determine whether our artwork, over the next many centuries, will be worthy of being remembered and appreciated. - *

1.17

On Artists

Artists of the past were crafstmen, artisans - into surviving - making profits, not striving to be prophets. . . - 2014 *

Painting, from the day we are born, does not make us an artist. It simply makes us someone who paints because we love to. - 2014 *

A female visual artist can sculpt and paint the female figure and child form to her hearts content and never have her sexual orientation questioned. A man's orientation and motives, on the other hand (if his subject matter is the male - adult or child) always are. - 2014 *

When everything is art, nothing is. When everyone is an artist, no one is. - 2013 *

A $100 watercolour sable no more makes an artist than a $10,000 camera makes a photographer. - 2013 *

As a painter my greatest need is to know that I don't know what it is that I always crave to know. And so I paint. - 2013 *

The less visual artists say about their work, the more intelligent it appears to be. - 2011 *

It is a compliment to be called an artist even though most people have no idea what or who an artist really is. But once this compliment has been offered, the recipient should simply say thank you and nothing else - lest the complimentor discover they have made a serious mistake. - 2009 *

The day visual artists begin to paint beyond their own self absorption, a renaissance of world wide magic will occur. - 2009 *

The goal of a successful hobbyist is to have fun. The goal of a professional is to be challenged over and over and over. - 2009 *

Talent speaks to the poetry of a visual artist's soul, skill - his or her capacity to speak well enough that viewers only see the talent. - 2009 *

In contemporary terms "I am an artist" is more often than not a speculative statement. - 2007 *

It is increasingly difficult to know what, if anything, a painting or sculpture is saying for the simple reason that the god-damned "artists" won't shut up! - 2007 *

Aux jeunes soi-disant artistes, je dis – peignez sans mettre l'accent sur vos détresses ou vos nombrils. Le devoir d'un peintre n'est pas *de s'afficher ou de chigner, mais de peindre, de rendre vrai ce que vous observez, ce que vous expérimentez, ce qui vous et nous touche. Votre rôle n'en est pas un de supériorité, mais plutôt celui de raconteur avisé. Enfin, dites-vous "peintres". C'est à la postérité de vous consacrer artiste. – 2007 **

The greatest insult to the visual arts is the capacity of some to so vociferously sell their lack of skill or talent as a "style". - 2007 *

Artists at times have difficulty saying what they mean because they are so used to feeling rather than thinking what they mean. - 2007 *

Since we live in times when the lowest common denominator often forms the basis of our culture and entertainment industries (and they are industries) many people who call themselves artists are not really lying or bragging. They simply have no idea that they are not. - 2006 *

If to draw, paint or sculpt we require the inspiration of an ever elusive muse most of our time will be spent doing nothing. - 2006 *

I don't call myself an artist because what if. . . what if I discover one day that I am not. Better to be known as a damned good painter than to be discovered a fraud. - 2006 *

Ce n'est pas aux artistes-peintres de prêcher la foi, mais de permettre au monde de découvrir la leur. - 2006 *

An artist is never threatened by technological innovation. That would be akin to giving a paint brush or chisel the same importance as creative potential. - 2005 *

Prostitute is what a non-selling painter calls another who's work does sell. - 2005 *

Artists, at their most poetic, do not create because they suffer. They create despite the fact that they may. - 2005 *

Quite often, the public sees a painter or sculptor's work as "not" work - in essence a hobby activity. And that, at times, is difficult to take. But more annoying are those who, purporting to be artists, seem incapable of fathoming that a person earning their living painting and sculpting works every day. They are not available, at the drop of a hat, for coffee chats or congenial visits to yet another local gallery. - 2005 *

Art is the essence of humanity as expressed by one whose need to reach out and touch is greater than his or her need to be touched. 2004 *

Feelings may grow from within but they are born from without; born of experience and community, from emotions and connections felt - both hard-edged and feathered.
The expression of feelings is what is born from within - to be reconnected to that which is without. For those inner feelings, when disconnected, are nothing more than emotions in greater need of expression than feeling; more in need of being heard than listened to.
We painters should take heed lest our visual screams be perceived too stridently vapid to be taken seriously. - 2001 *

Artistic statements are far too often a combination of incoherent psychobabble blended with pseudo-intellectual nonsense to be taken seriously. More desperate cries for recognition than insightful presentation, statements mean little if anything to a legitimate collector. - 2001 *

There has to be more to the visual arts than me, myself and I. - 2001 *

A woman visual artist who creates artwork extraordinarily well is not a great "female visual artist". By the very fact that her work is extraordinary we should simply refer to her as a great visual artist. - 2001 *

As with every other element in the creation of artwork, the proportion and positioning of a signature is vital in that when it is too big or too small, it speaks more to the insecurity of the visual artist than to the work itself. - 2001 *

*On ne peut être artiste visuel sans pouvoir se mettre dans la peau de l'autre; ressentir ses peines et ses joies, ses triomphes et défaites. L'artiste visuel est l'interprète du vrai. Et, il n'y a pas de vrais sans un partage du tout de la vie. - 2001 **

Purportedly, contemporary artwork is all about having something to say and saying it. And yet, very few contemporary visual artists have anything to say except that they have something to say - and would we all "just please shut up and listen!!!". - 2000 *

Self- expression has no redeeming value if it is not tempered by self-discipline.- 1999 *

deKooning was the only true "disposable-art" artist. He was both the author of its creation and of its evolution and demise. So many have tried to imitate his process, (which they have inevitably failed to grasp, or ever once truly imitated). In this, deKooning remains unique and will forever be. - 1998 *

I would no more reply to the question : "And what do you do for a living?" with the answer : "I am a genius" - anymore than I would appropriate the title "artist". I am a proud painter like any dancer is proud to dance or violinist proud to play. I leave the superlatives (or not) to viewers. - 1998 *

The spirituality of Peter Max is what is missing in much of today's paintings. - 1998 *

How sad it is that, today, being an artist seems so much more important than doing artwork. - 1998 *

Style becomes irrelevant, becomes the lowest common denominator factor of an end-product when we allow our obsession with it to disturb the purity of the process. - 1998 *

When one hundred or so people gather for cocktails, visual artists in the crowd are easy to spot. They're the ones thoroughly engrossed by a speck of reflected light emanating from some indistinguishable form, surrounded by the inky blackness of a narrow space created by a slightly open door of an adjacent much more intriguing room. - 1998 *

Romantics and artists are undoubtedly the most difficult people to live with. Artists because they love their work more than life itself. Romantics because they are willing to suffer 75% of their lives in order to anticipate the pleasures which must assuredly await them in the 25% left over. - 1998 *

Of those who wear the crown of "artist" before the coronation, be wary. - 1997 *

If art is to ever again be respected, the definition of a contemporary artist, must be redefined to mean : one who expresses thoughts and feelings in such a unique way that despite the wildest of "ism-atic" leanings, and the generalized homogenization of public perceptions, the initial integrity of his or her expression is not only sustained but forever nurtured and evolving. - 1997 *

There are too many "artists" in this world and not enough sketchers, painters and sculptors. - 1997 *

It takes a brave soul to tread the path well worn by previous painters, sculptors and other visual artists. Wishing to be an artist means accepting it as a long term dream with multiple short term goals. For most of our lives will be spent honing the skills needed to realize such a dream. And perhaps. . . for a very short and precious moment, its pleasurable realization may be ours. . . or maybe not - 1997 *

2.7

If I announce, despite lack of qualification and peer acknowledgement, a decision to practice medicine, I would soon be sent to prison. Yet, if I choose to "be" an artist - even worse, an art teacher - (despite a glaring lack of credentials, or professional peer recognition) I am applauded without question and envied my "talent", my daring, my creativity. . . Such is the level to which we have relegated artistic expression in our times. - 1997 *

Professional maturity is evident only in the individual who transcends his personal haunts and delves, rather, into the world's collective encounters, preoccupations and anxieties; both positive and negative, real and imagined. - 1996 *

The goal of too many visual artists is the attainment of proficiency in the writing of grant applications. - 1996 *

An artist is an interpretive voyeur who, once spurred into expressing that which stimulates his mind's eye, deliberately creates with astonishing clarity a vision totally unique to his person, yet mesmerizing to a collective of viewers. - 1995 *

Human activity in the realm of the visual arts has several levels of proficiency :

Basic interest:

A basic interest in art is one where someone is intrigued, goes to an exhibition, enjoys his/her time there but will not relate to it on any other level than a once in a while "aesthetically appealing" (or not) activity.

Hobby (Amateur):

The word "amateur" is French with a Latin origin. "Amo" (I love). To be called an amateur, is not an insult. It simply means we love art. In contemporary terms, though, amateur has come to mean a hobbyist who loves art but is more interested in the perfectionism of results than in true craftsmanship or self-expression.

Craftsman:

A craftsman is one who has an affinity for the results elicited by his/her efforts - but this at a high level of rendering. A craftsman finds the process culminating in a beautifully rendered product intriguing. The stamp of a good craftsman is his/her ability to repeat quality achievement. The best take craftsmanship to an artistic level.

Artist:

Artists are passionate individuals who have a deep appreciation and respect for technical expertise (craftsmanship) which is an exercise in the honing of the skills required to speak the artistic visual language of their choice. Artists by internalizing a language's essence and elements free themselves to "uniquely" and clearly self-express in such a way that communication between the finished work of art and the viewer is not only possible but inevitable and incredible. Few of us ever reach this level. But it's fun trying! - 1995 *

The role of artists has never been to make the world a better place. Their task is more akin to holding a mirror up to the world and letting it decide for itself what it is that needs doing. - 1995 *

Without dissatisfaction it is impossible to create... Only souls searching for a better space can foster the necessary drive to renew themselves. - 1995 *

At fifty I have no need to anxiously please or shock like a twenty year old feels he must. At fifty I don't need to "explain" or decipher my work. At fifty, I can paint what I damned well please without justifying each brushstroke. How wonderful it is to be an "old fart" painter. - 1995 *

Je suis de Venise. . . Et je ne le suis pas.
Comme elle, mes sources ne sont pas tout à fait claires.
Tous deux, nous sommes d'origines mixtes.
Comme elle, je suis païen tout en étant chrétien, latin, tout en étant barbare.
Comme elle, j'ai le coeur byzantin, le sang arabe,
l'âme grecque et la voix grégorienne.
Comme tous les Francos, je n'ai pas vraiment de chez-moi.
Je m'adapte donc aux caresses mythiques et mystiques de celle qui m'attire.
Je suis donc nourrissons de mère Venise.
À sa poitrine je suis chez moi. Ailleurs, je ne suis qu'en exil. - 1995
*

Why do we fear creative women? It seems we do. The world still raises girls with more expectations and rules than for boys. Their voice is always honed to be more "socially acceptable", silenced at times; more rigidly associated with the aims of perfection than the freedoms inherent in a quest for excellence. Are our expectations based on a deeply rooted need to see them more as beautiful than "do" beautifully?

There is nothing so wondrous than a child exploding with creative potential - knowing deep down inside that she is free to be so. But, from early on girls sense there is, for them, a cultural, "societal limitations" rule book - one which lays out her predetermined "girl's" path, for no other reason than she is "a girl". She can watch and appreciate and even "try" creativity but she should nonetheless not stray too far from the rule book dictums. That would make her different somehow. . .

Are we afraid of those differences? Are we afraid, they might make our wives, mothers daughters, sisters "different"? Too easily resemble Mary Cassatt, Diana Krall, Ely Kish, Louise Bourgeois, Aretha Franklin, Artemisia Gentileschi, Emily Carr, Louise Vigée Lebrun, KD Lang, Camille Claudel?

They grew up "different". They became different than our expectations. Thank God for that. - 1993 *

The language used by artists to translate perceptions into a tangibly scrumptious image depends on the energies emitted by the subject, the interpretation the artists seek to transmit and the fluency with which they implement their chosen mode of expression. - 1990 *

I am a painter because I paint. I am an artist only because others say I am. - 1989 *

Lorsqu'on n'a que onze ans et qu'on travaille depuis déjà plusieurs années pour réaliser le rêve de sa vie - c'est à dire : devenir artiste

2.11

- on a du chemin à faire... Mais on ne le sait pas.
C'est ça avoir le coeur d'enfant; avoir le coeur d'artiste.
Quand on a 45 ans et qu'on est toujours à rêver les mêmes rêves,
c'est parceque en vérité on a toujours onze ans. . . Mais cette fois-
ci, on le sait.
Et c'est alors qu'on découvre la différence entre ceux qui ont
toujours été artistes et ceux qui, malheureusement, ne le seront
jamais. - 1989 *

I don't "look like" an artist because I don't know what an artist is supposed to look like. I would rather strive to become one than waste my time and energy trying to convince others, (or even myself), that I look like or "am" one. - 1988 *

The moment individuals entitle themselves "artist", presumes (or imposes upon others) that the "artwork" produced is "art". - 1984 *

A visual artist does not do artwork to be recognized but to maintain the enjoyment of discovery and creativity in his own soul and to hold onto the "wonder" upon which that creativity thrives. Nevertheless, no one objects to recognition or its concomitant side-effect of being able to pay off the mortgage. - 1979 *

Once an artwork is completed, a creator should not presume that they remain relevant to the continuing existence of that artwork. - 1978 *

The only difference between me (a painter) and my father (a mechanic) is the oil on our hands. - 1976*

One day, hopefully far far away,
when I am a painter old and grey,
I will have the maturity to shut up
when I no longer have anything to say. - 1967 *

Propaganda is never art, nor art propaganda. If anything, expressions of this ilk are nothing more than mind graffiti, imposed advertising, promotion and marketing of the worst kind - and this by the least sensitive of those who value no other thought or need than their own. - *

The only true value of a work of art is measured in the market place. - (Renoir) *

To be an artist is not to elevate myself above the fray but rather to elevate myself above myself. -*

Personal style is an inevitable by-product of the creative process. Though it is something about which we are remotely conscious, the minute we search for "it", worry about it, anxiously probe it or try to emphasize its uniqueness or discuss its relevance - it is instantly demeaned by our need to "control" it. - *

A contemporary problem in the visual arts is the obsessive need for recognition and validation - a pleading for beatification even before death. We should beware of that which we wish for. - *

No one simply wants to paint or sculpt anymore. In that, many of today's visual artists reflect the generic roots of the narcissistic society from which they come. - *

2.13

Finally, all depends on oneself. It is the sun of a thousand rays in the belly. All else is nothing. - (Picasso) *

The 21st cent is the beginning of a new era, hopefully, where Peck's Bad Boy antics will remain in the art school hallways where they belong - with graduates, hopefully, moving on to greater maturity and aspirations. - *

Dipping a brush into the crevices of one's navel rarely, if ever, induces inspiration or a result worthy of the time and effort required to look at it; let alone appreciate it. - *

An artist wonders more about what he does not know than about what he does. - *

That a painter or sculptor would take the time and effort to apprentice, to practice, to work, to forge ahead, to strive to achieve a goal of self-sufficiency is a much older ideation than that of becoming a bohemian romantic starving for his or her "art". - *

A piano player is a hobbyist. A student of the piano an apprentice. A pianist is a trained technician good enough to please an audience with borrowed imagery. An artist is a professional who not only dazzles with imagery in a most sensual way; he or she does so even if the piano being played has only three working keys. - *

On April 30, 1896, Cézanne wrote to Joachim Gasquet: *"All my life I have worked to be able to earn my living, but I thought that one could do good painting without attracting attention to one's private life. Certainly, an artist wishes to raise himself intellectually as*

2.14

*much as possible, but the man must remain obscure. The pleasure must be found in the work." - ***

Prince Charles will undoubtedly be a good King. As a painter he has learned that the process, the concept of ever-learning, holds more riches than the becoming or the being. - *

An artist is simply a vehicle through which an emerging vision passes. - *

Begin by drawing and painting like the old masters; after that, do as you like - you will always be respected. - (Dali) *

Conversing (visually) with an audience demands that we respect ourselves and our partner in conversation. As a visual artist, screaming at or self-indulgent posturing are adolescent tools meant to belittle, to subordinate, to obfuscate and to abuse an audience we consider less intelligent than we are. The reverse is most often true. - *

Figurative artists practice a craft which elevates creative effort to its ancient heights, i.e.: artists work hard at creating concrete evidence of man's search for validity, connection, adaptation and survival. - *

Narcissistically applied daubs of paint may appear esoterically complex at times; imitating intellectuality. . . therefore logicality? Therefore art? For whom is this so? No one seems to have a clue. - *

2.15

*Si les jeunes peintres travaillaient aussi fort pour créer des oeuvres de qualité qu'ils travaillent fort à se faire reconnaître artiste . . . ***

So many loudly proclaim themselves "artist", discoursing profusely on the lack of recognition of "their art".
So few proudly discuss the intricacies and grandeur of "craftsmanship", of the passion and energizing thrusts which lead them to simply and humbly say "I paint". - *

L'art de bouder et de taper du pied est né d'un intense besoin de se faire remarquer lorsqu'on n'a ni les moyens ni le talent de se faire comprendre.

Notes explicatives:

> *"L'art de bouder et de taper du pied" signifie qu'on est centré sur nos propres besoins sans reconnaître l'existence et l'importance de "l'autre".*
> *"Intense besoin" signifie une expression frénétique, née d'un sentiment d'impuissance provenant non pas d'un manque d'avoir quelque chose à dire, mais plutôt d'un manque d'apprentissage qui aurait pu faciliter l'expression des sentiments et/ou observations.*

> *"Se faire remarquer" signifie un besoin désordonné, né d'un malentendu qui semble donner au peintre l'idée que l'accent de son expression est lui-même.*

> *"Pas les moyens de se faire comprendre" présupposent qu'un*

apprentissage de piètres qualités a permis au jeune apprenti de croire son expression artistique plus importante que la nécessité d'assimiler le métier: c à d : le langage : son orthographe, sa grammaire, sa phraséologie.

N'ayant pas la capacité de communiquer une pensée ou un sentiment de façon professionnelle, la seule solution au monde des "voulant se faire appeler artistes", est d'accuser le peuple d'ignorance et de créer un jargon incompréhensible, propre seulement à ceux et celles qui acceptent l'ignorance comme talent.

Il faut tout de même savoir reconnaître sa place et la place de notre oeuvre dans un contexte de communication. L'accent est de transmettre un message compréhensif et tangible.

*Sans ça, on finit par parler fort, sans rien dire. - ***

Better to be seen to be a good enough painter than be discovered a wanting "artist". - *

How arrogant is the painter who purports his navel lint is more compelling, more enthralling than that of the viewer. - *

"Artists' statements" are, more often than not, better left unsaid. - *

An artist is someone who sees everything in nothing. *

Artists view life's eccentricities as the spice with which one flavours the soul. - *

2.17

Those who profess being artists rarely are. - *

Politicians are often remembered for who/what they tried to be, visual artists for what their work did or did not say. - *

That we can look and hear does not mean we see or listen. - *

We should never expect to be an artist - or need to be seen to be one. We can only legitimately aspire to achieve such a goal, to hope that such an "appointment" will one day be ours. All is in the hands of an adoring, or not, public. - *

If it is selfish to be introspective and self probing, wanting to correct and better one's own feelings and observations rather than to attack the differences in others... than, yes, the artist is a self-centred individual. - *

Though visual artists are often viewed as a dissatisfied lot, they suffer much less than those who feel caught up in a world they can't stand, can't or won't change, can't or will not deal with. The bad or variant moods of visual artists are very often expressions of accumulated frustration; faced as they are with a world which refuses to acknowledge there are solutions to the problems in which society seems to enjoy wallowing. - *

Painters who need as much recognition as their work are like parents unwilling to "free" their children at the time they should be let go - selfishly afraid the children will not be worthy of their efforts, anxious that they, and not their offspring will be judged poorly. . . - *

2.18

The interpretation of artwork is the viewer's prerogative. If the painter feels compelled to explain what has been "said", just maybe, it was not stated quite clearly enough. - *

Money makes a visual artist's life easier... not better. - *

Screaming isn't enough. You have to have something to say. - *

*Lorsqu'un peintre fait des "crises à l'enfant perturbé" aussi facilement qu'un chef cuisinier ses tartines, il va sans dire que le premier se fera rejeter, le deuxième louanger. - **

Artists both crave and dread recognition. They do what they do despite the pressure and fear of it. For, to the true of heart the need to "do" artwork is ever more stronger than the need to "be seen " to be an artist. - *

The artist's role is to observe and take note... not to judge or denigrate. - *

The wearing of a Detroit Tigers baseball cap does not a player make. - *

The title of art or artist should never be absconded with nor should either title be bestowed upon anyone or anything which is less than incredible. - *

How is it possible to differentiate between an "up and coming visual artist" and one who is not? The answer is simple: The one to respect speaks of his work, the other of himself. - *

The need to be called an artist is to crave being perceived as wonderfully as we would wish our artwork truly was. - *

A painter is only true to herself when her message relates more to the universe than to herself. - *

*L'artiste visuel contemporain se vante trop facilement d'être bon "quêteux". - **

Visual artists wishing to be remembered posthumously with fanfare and praise should hope to make enough money during their lifetime to buy up their total career production - this in order to cull and destroy anything which might taint that dreamed-of status. - *

Recognition is a two-edged sword. It allows us to forge ahead with confidence whilst constantly nipping at our heels to be fed. - *

If I become rich because I paint, that is wonderful. If I do not become rich because I paint, that is also wonderful. - *

When the name of a painter is more renown than the work she has created;.when the name is more easily remembered than the poetry she has written - it speaks of one of two things: either a decline in the work's true value or the painter is dead. - *

In any pursuit it is pleasant to recognize that one's efforts please. And yet, the fact that they do is a wondrously incidental happening which does nothing more than indicate we have not lost our connection with the world. But, should we ever expect to please, our goals become tainted; losing their intrinsic value. - *

2.20

For centuries, the work of artists has been the mirror of society. Today, those who claim the title more often than not see only themselves reflected. - *

How much richer is a life producing artwork which, once we are gone, continues to speak eloquently on its own. - *

It is better that a visual artist die later in life than be eulogized by the less objective remnants of his own generation. To wish for entry into the pantheon, an adequate amount of mourning time and oblivion are required as it takes later, less subjective generations to rediscover, or not, the master qualities, or lack thereof, of those who came before. - *

Poor maligned Lucian Freud. Though he fit the neurotic mould of his illustrious predecessor, he certainly was much less dangerous to the world than that predecessor. Lucian was rather passionate about specific body representations which both repel and attract. He seemed to relish in the display of exaggerated "normal imperfections". But how is this more bizarre than the body-phobic obsessions in our times and the allure of anorexia as a benchmark for perfection?
Granted. The artist was an eccentric. But then, that rendered him more endearing, not crazier.
Today, the English speaking world seems to want to rid itself of these fascinating individuals. In our Google enlightenment era, we consider anything out of the ordinary perverted and sneaky whereas such individuals are rather nothing more than loners wanting to simply be who they are without intervention by those of us who "know better".

What a boring world we are becoming. What a dangerous censorship oriented realm we are becoming. Too much self-righteous beatification and too many inquisitions going on via witch-hunts. Not enough righteous respect and appreciation of differences are available in our era to allow ourselves a definition of enlightened times.

As for Freud's painting style, if style it be, his compositions were intricate and very "genres" - in that they told stories - something which is rather rare today. And when attempted, contemporary painter stories are often poorly told. We seem to have lost the capacity to say something visually meaningful.

And because Freud's "tales" are intricate, our lack of sophistication frustrates our comprehension and so we demean his intent.

That Lucian Freud probably painted the "body-ugly" as a reminder of life's fleeting beauty is more plausible than his perceptions were awry. Was he possibly reminding himself and us that his body visions are rather akin, in these rather bizarre times, to how we see them : sinful, horrid, and rather putrid -thus not to be touched? Was he saying that our perceived ugliness was only good for self-abuse and that (to ourselves at least) in a weirdly titillating way? Me thinks he was a better, more humane psychiatrist than his grand-father. He's told us more about ourselves in visual parlance than grand-papa ever did with his million self-serving revisionist words. - *

On Craft

Being skilled in the use of a language does not guarantee we are poets, novelists or biographers. It simply makes us skilled. A true poet, painter, pianist sculptor, videographer is one who takes his or her language beyond the ordinary, beyond the skill, beyond basic comprehension and analysis. - 2015 *

Does training in the visual arts mean following traditional rules of anatomical study, cast reproduction and academically regulated exercises? Do diplomas in the arts have value? Not necessarily. Training means knowing of and how to implement, however the knowledge has been obtained, the basic elements of composition, drawing, painting, sculpture and other disciplines associated with visual representation. Without these no language can be spoken which has the capability of carrying the weight of the demands we put upon it. - 2015 *

Apprenticeship is about learning skills. Craft about proving the skills have been assimilated. Artwork is about playing creatively with those skills. Art about giving that creativity wings. - 2014 *

The only rule a visual arts teacher must promote is that students can break all the rules they want as long as, beforehand, they learn and assimilate and understand fully the rules they wish to break. - 2011 *

The ultimate goal of learning a skill is to integrate it, master it so completely we never have to think about it again. - 2007 *

Without skill artwork may occur but never art. - 2007 *

Only in the visual arts, it seems, can a lack of talent and technical skill be described as a "personal style". - 2007 *

To so-called art teachers who say there is only one rule in drawing and painting and that is that there are no rules, I say: Please stop insulting those who are real teachers and ruining the futures of eager students.. - 2007 *

If we fail to recognize or refuse to acknowledge "craft" in art - if we deny the acquisition of skill as crucial – we place ourselves in a position of never achieving beyond our own ignorance. – 1997 *

To express ourselves artistically it is necessary, beforehand, to know of the history, knowledge and discipline of the crafts which serve as the conduits for that expression. - 1983 *

The expression of creative thought is impossible without the discipline of craft. Without it, expression is but a spoiled pretty child forever demanding attention. - 1978*

Only an assimilated self-discipline can support the wild abandon of free creative expression. - 1967 *

Dance, music or writing for the most part remain vital artistic expressions because they have never rejected, destroyed or scoffed at the root disciplines of their very foundations.

The visual arts, on the other hand, have long ago abandoned the "playing of scales", replaced freedom of expression with licence and promoted "rights" over "privilege".

When no spelling, grammar or syntax a once universal language becomes alien, incomprehensible, uncommunicative and of no intrinsic value to anybody other than to the hermitage unskilled "artists" have come to embrace as their own. - *

How ironic that during an era whose quality of technical training is at an all time high, the quality of visual arts training is at an all time low. - *

Today "craft", the core of grammar and spelling in all visual expressions, no longer presides over what constitutes contemporary artistic and creative expression. In its place stands the one exclusive element which now dominates and defines the expression of creativity: "moi". - *

3.4

On Creativity

Creativity is the greatest enemy of conformity, of total obedience and of submission to political correctness. It dares when authoritarian initiatives demand it dare not. - 2015 *

So many envy those who are considered creative - for being able to leave something of value to the world. So many times, I walk away from such comments, thanking God I am not one of their children. - 2014

Though many creative types are silenced by the environments in which they find themselves, many are silenced by those in which they confine themselves. - 2013 *

Creative individuals do not wonder about being creative. They create. Those who concentrate on "wanting" to be rarely are. - 2011 *

Creative individuals are those who when they fail do not feel destroyed. - 2010 *

If truth be told, the greatest financial outlay related to establishing creative potential is in providing children with healthy food and adequate sleep. - 2010 *

The best parents do not tell their children to be something. They tell them to do something. - 2005 *

A growing common inability to differentiate between passion and obsession is a key element identifying an era's growing lack of creativity. - 2004 *

If I was half as curious as my cat Laurier, I would be a thousand times more creative. - 2002 *

It is the glass half empty or half full; the thick darkness of night or a rich, deep backdrop to the stars. When emptiness cries out in despair, creativity sings the praises of the invisibility of air. - 2002 *

Even a child perceived to have limited potential has more creative energy than most of us will ever hope to have after the age of sixteen. - 2002 *

It is generally by the least creative person in a room that pleasurable musings are disturbed - dreams being considered a waste of time, no more valuable than fluttering butterflies or annoying moths to be swatted and got rid of as soon as possible. - 2001 *

How rigidly we perceive the world and how flexible and fearless we are in applying ourselves to dealing with our findings,

4.2

determines to what degree we are open to artistic interpretation. - 2001 *

The constant craving to render easy everything we do is the very act by which we ultimately destroy all vestiges of human creative potential. - 2001 *

I would rather fail than wonder "what if". Sometimes, trying is the only proof we are truly, deliciously alive. - 1999 *

The world will see better days when there is less craving for the next new product and more appreciation for the process of creation which brought about the existence of products already in hand. - 1998 *

Without the mind's eye, truth becomes absolute, facts infallible, creativity impossible, innovation obsolete, discovery implausible and stagnation inevitable. - 1997 *

By the age of 10 or 11 many children have lost their innate curiosity to question, to scrutinize, to experiment, to find pleasure in discovery. Already afraid of failure, of not being good enough, their adult-like resignation is excruciatingly palpable. - 1996 *

Creativity does not exist without difficulties and most of all without eccentricity. When it does, it is not creativity. And without creativity there is no passion, and without that - no life. And this is why homogenization in races and cultures, governments and the arts is the devastating virus that it is. - 1995 *

To generically render ourselves safe within the bosom of sameness is to sit back - to await the only thing which is possible to create in such an environment : extinction. - 1995 *

Production is often mistaken for creativity and licence for freedom of expression. - 1991 *

An evolved society is one which channels its primal urges into the total fulfilment of creative impulses. - 1989 *

The Creator, in asking us to be childlike, never once saw us as dependent, innocent, naïve, or submissive - those qualities attributed to children by controlling adult figures. Rather, God created us and wished us vibrant, curious, giving, daring, caring, questioning. . . and most of all creative. - 1983 *

*Only through imitation do we develop toward originality. - (John Steinbeck) - 1902-1968 - *

*Add a pinch of hope to a state of oppression and you have creativity - Louis Dudeck) *

No curiosity should go unsated, lest the discovery of the mystery of mysteries be inadvertently overlooked. - *

Creative thinkers are fascinated by the infinite directions a thought process can take. Logical thinkers are baffled by its laterality. At worst, they are fearful; critical and vengeful when confronted by it. And, oddly always, they are envious of those who flow into and through and out of it. - *

The creative process should never be easy. Comfortable, yes. Easy, never. - *

To acknowledge that the struggle between the urges of creativity and destructiveness is the true essence of man is to recognize that we are responsible for our own salvation, evolution and inevitable demise. - *

Étrange... Quoique la créativité soit seule vraie source de liberté elle en est autant plus seule vraie source de sécurité. - *

The soul of a creative individual never dies. Only collective normality dies. - *

Rebels are those who go against the grain no matter what. The 20th century's visual art rebels must therefore have been its figurative painters and sculptors. - *

To be truly alive is to create, to judge no other, to live judiciously and to be free of domination. *

When the infinite vastness of a child's creativity is realized, we can only weep at the loss of childhood. - *

Artistic expression allows those who feel imposed upon by the most rigid edges of society to speak freely and without guilt - *

If to be creative we must await the inspiration of an ever elusive muse, we will spend most of our lives doing nothing. - *

The factual mind is the tool of an academic intellect whose sole purpose is the simplification, codification and facilitation of the accumulation and assimilation of information . *

When compensation is mistaken for satisfaction, creativity is eroded. - *

Boredom is either a door through which one passes to reach the complete darkness and paralysis of despair or through which one discovers the tingling attraction and sensual pleasure of a creative response to the nothing that boredom emits. - *

Passion is essential if personal aspirations are ever to be achieved. Sad are those who have no concept of it. Sadder still those who perceive passion as obsession. Theirs is a world of illusions. - *

Creative expression is often at its greatest when in reaction to suppression, oppression or one's inability to accept that the norm is all there is. - *

On Critiquing & Criticizing

An unsolicited critique is more often than not a criticism by a self-anointed authority -2013 *

Never rely on a critic to tell you what is right or wrong with a painting. Let the painting tell its story. Let it tell you well or poorly. Let the legacy of the last brush stroke whisper in your ear. Let the technical prowess, the craftsmanship amaze you. Let the burnt sienna wash below the sap green and alizarin transparencies create a tingling sensation in your spine - one that is only possible when the richest and deepest connections are made between two kindred spirits. . . a painter and a viewer.

Sit before a painting and let it enter you and let yourself enter it. Let the communion embrace the totality that is the blend of giver and receiver - never knowing, after awhile, which is which. Let the painting tell you its most intimate secrets - if it can. Let the painting love you - if it will, and you it - if you can.

But never let anyone steal away with that which is intimately yours. For today's critics/censors know little about so much and so much about so little. - 2012 - *

Judgements are often made in the blind corner of the world where criticism passes for wisdom. - 2004 *

By colouring within the lines, I discovered acceptance. By colouring without, freedom. - 1981 *

It is so much easier to paint a wall than try your hand at creating a masterpiece. The former chore critics ignore. The latter daring they inevitably attack. - *

*The jealousy of unsuccessful painters will be the thermometer of your success. - (Dali) - **

Censorship is an imposition of conformity to rules arbitrarily established by individuals and groups who have no intention of ever being subjected to the demands they impose upon others. - *

*Don't judge me by the books I read But by the use I make of knowledge - (Anon) - **

On Design

Design, that facet of life which extols the virtues of balance and rhythm and flow and movement and life. - 2015 *

Most contemporary room design errs in that it is based on the object of it rather than the space - the environment of it. - 2012 *

Design would be so much better if it actually was about "design" rather than being the latest aberrant topic on reality TV. - *

Design is just like... no, actually, it is identical to painting, creating comics, writing, music, movies, architecture, street lamps and magic. As I work at my craft with both effort and thought, imaginary borders between all "mediums" (and isms) fade.
The whole thing is revealed to be a series of vehicles identical in nature: all are lenses or mirror-like tools which channel and/or reflect radiating clusters and patterns of energy that we either communicate at best with uncanny clarity of purpose, or send out as ill noise in the name of aesthetic tricks that make sense at the time - but fail for lack of better craft.

*The real "trick", it seems, is composition according to the solid core of classical ideals which support the best expression. It is here that aesthetics are born. - (Dominic Bercier, visual artist, story-teller) - ** *

A quality designer is one who considers who the client is and how that client lives. Coupled with that information, a professional's ability and talents should be enough to create an environment which highlights the wishes of the client - and not their own. - *

If I am the client and my preference is for the colour Ultramarine Blue. . . I don't want to be sold on the merits of Pthalo. Design with my blue or I'll find someone who can. (I think a smiley face - with gritted teeth - would add much to this comment) - *

In centuries past, visual artists and designers created to meet the needs of clients - be they individuals, institutions, or governments. Despite this pressure to accommodate such a diverse and demanding clientele, the world's art and environmental design flourished to a level of excellence - yet to be replicated or maintained in our times. - *

On Drawing

In the beginning of time, simple drawings were the first reflection of the pains and joys of life. The only utterances required were probably in line with a recognition sound like : "aw". Without words, those drawings would have said all that needed saying.

With evolution, we began drawing more and more complex reactions to ourselves and to the world around us. And "aw" no longer met the needs of the new capacities we had. Wonder turned to questioning, and questioning again to further wonder.

In essence, when words were impossible, drawings explained us to ourselves. But the more we evolved, the more our drawings "said" and the more we learned and the more we wanted to know. And because we did, our minds began questioning again. And the more we did the more we wanted to understand. And so we finally uttered our first question. And so, born of "aw", what and who and how and when came to be.

How wondrous is that, that without drawing there would never have been any reason for minds to wonder, for words to exist, for questions to be asked. Take that ye deniers of the value of the visual arts. (Wink.) - 2015 *

If there is something wrong with the nose, check the cheeks; something wrong with the mouth, check the chin and upper lip. Anything else wrong? Start over again. . . - 2014 *

Lines, good or bad, are more often than not the legitimate founders of an initial visualized thought. And because they are, they may frighten. Why? Because lines tell many truths. And because they do, they are often crushed into oblivion beneath smears and blankets of aggressive paint. Yet. . . swimming under and within those thick hues and tints and shades, is the determination of those lines. . . daring the paint to drown them. . . In the end, lines always win. The structure determines the essence of an artwork – not surface artifice. - 2011*

Lines are the foundation within which shapes take form – for the eye to see and the soul to feel. . . And this they must achieve with just the right timing, and intensity and positioning amongst all of the other elements within a compositional stage play – within which, expected or not, they speak vividly their "lines". -2011 *

We in the art world would speak more eloquently, more poetically, more vividly if we would just "learn our lines". – 2011*

I studied drawing and painting for many years in order not to have to think of drawing and painting when I am drawing and painting. - 2007 *

The incredible idea that a speck. . . a dot extended suddenly becomes a line which, at the pace of a heart-beat - a soul search, has the power to sensuously and rhythmically become life is mind-boggling. - 2006 *

Drawing is not about where you wish to take a line but where you go once you have let the line take you out of yourself. - 1997 *

A line must have lilt, tact, brash élan, resonant rhythms and swashbuckling zest. It must soothe and excite, float and dive, soar and bellow, whisper and coo, cry and dream, bleat and roar, swear, smell, hate and adore. . . A line must be able to say it all. . . at just the right moment. . . or find itself lying flat and lifeless. - 1997 *

Lines are the structure, the direction, the movement of our visual stories. - *

Thumb nail sketches bare witness to the workings of the mind's eye as it sails through the millions of daily pickings arousing curiosity in those who are open to "what is possible" rather than simply to what is ruled acceptable. - *

The fear of drawing hands disappears the moment we are more awed by their intricacy, strength, beauty and warmth than we are by their complexity. - *

"When my daughter was about seven years old, she one day asked me what I did at work. I told her I worked at the college - that my job was to teach people how to draw. She stared at me, incredulous, and said, "You mean they forget?" - (Howard Ikemoto) *

For coloured pencils to be valid tools of expression they must first imitate, evolve and learn from their monochromatic cousins. - *

Used discretely, with frugality and foresight, a line says more than it does through exaggerated or extravagant displays of its potential. - *

The study of folds is simply a series of exercises, to be fondly repeated forever and ever.- *

On The Nude

Being comfortable in the nude means exactly that - that "we" are comfortable with our bodies. Therefore, being nude is more about how we see ourselves than how others see us.

How we dress inevitably makes a public statement about what and who we want people to think we are or profess to be.

Being naked, on the other hand, is how we never want to be seen, since more often than not we can't bare (!) to carry "that vision off" comfortably - and that says more about us than we want anybody to know. - 2015 *

*La journée où nous ne serons plus représentés dans le domaine des arts - sous la forme universelle du nu - sera le moment même du début et de notre déclin et de notre éventuelle extinction. - 2015 **

Oddly, humans are openly critical of their bodies - all too often finding them ugly. Yet, they so rarely attack the integrity of their souls in the same manner. - 2015 *

Pas étonnant, mais toujours incroyable, qu'aujourd'hui le miracle du corps humain n'est que cochonnerie à être caché aux yeux des enfants - quoique la violence, elle, n'est rien de plus qu'un simple atout aux sports modernes et/ou un sujet grossièrement répété 24 heures par jour par les médias. (Pourquoi pas? C'est payant.) - 2015 *

A real nude is not afraid to be nude. It doesn't sport a "cache sex". When it does, all the emphasis is directed to the "offending" organs rather than the vision, the statement, the pure essence of a presence, an action, a movement, a rhythm.

A created nude which either negates the existence of the genital area through "erasing" or highlights it by covering only "that" area emphasizes nothing more than "nakedness"; turning what is right and good into a frightening or sinful thing. How risible and yet how sad we are, that upon looking at ourselves in the mirror, all we see is fear and evil. - 2015 *

Aujourd'hui, le corps humain n'est rien de plus qu'un outil d'annonce publicitaire, soit pour les maillots de bain, les autos, les produits de beauté - soit pour nous rappeler qu'il est déficient sans le prochain bistouri, la prochaine pilule de jouvence. - 2015 *

Le nu, on peut en faire ce que l'on veut. Mais, plus souvent que jamais, ce qu'il est en vérité c'est tout à fait autre chose. - 2015 *

How more calming it is to look upon a nude - not as defrocked and naked but as natural and glorious as the Creator wished it; rendered it. - 2014 *

You know it is too cold in the studio for the nude model when you discover yourself focused on the rendering of goose bumps. - 2012
*

One of the most refreshing discoveries to be made in painting the human form is that there is no such thing as skin colour – just varied forms and shapes continuously affected and altered by the hue and tonal implications of other surfaces reflecting the ambient warm and/or cool light sources in the figure's environment. - 2010
*

Would it not be rather arrogant, rather self-aggrandizing as a lowly human, to stand before God and to tell him to His face; to bluntly stipulate that His most complex and incredibly enigmatic creation is a fuck-up? - 2009 *

If anything, the vast majority of contemporary painters and sculptors of the figure are nothing short of universal in their level of expertise: i.e. : they know next to nothing about surface anatomy, and it shows. (To break the rules we must first know the rules.) - 2007 *

There is too much self-loathing in the contemporary nude figure for it to be considered anything but naked. - 2006 *

Naked is a collective moral issue, nude an individual physical, emotional well being consideration. - 2006 *

It is not possible to appreciate the incredible wondrous construct, story-telling curves, movements and rhythms of the nude human body unless the one displaying it for us (through drawing, painting, sculpture or photography) has the skills and talent to see above and

8.3

beyond the scratching, sniffling and wheezing physicality of nakedness.

To limit the human body to nothing more than skin and sinew relativity and mechanics is to relegate it to the self-loathing ramifications which now dictate the depressed mentality of our times. – 2005 *

The most soul tingling of exercises is to look upon the full nude figure of the human form and to dig into it with one's eye until there is nothing else alive but the scratch of chalk to paper and a sudden muscle twitch - not ours, not the subject's but rather that of the newly sketched form on the drawing surface. - 1992 *

It is not that the nude or nudity is disturbing, but that we are disturbed by it which is revealing. - 1985 *

*To delight in the human body without shame, to enjoy it without adulteration, is no simple human prerogative. It comes only at the summit of a high culture. - (Lewis Mumford - American historian and critic) - 1895-1990 - *

At any age, the body beautiful is not one which is large or small, tall or short, wide or thin, young or old. Rather a wondrous body is balanced. There is equilibrium between the length and width and depth and height of each part and all parts harmonious to the whole. - 1983 *

When I can repeatedly stir the soul through the three-dimensional intensity of a leg, from groin to ankle; via a sketch of only one line, stretched from the top of a drawing surface to the bottom edge, then and only then, has the moment arrived when I may call myself artist, master, teacher. Until then, I am nothing in the art of being an artist. - 1978 *

Il y a tellement de haine de soi dans les nus contemporains qu'il est difficile de ne pas les considérer rien de plus que "tout nu". - *

Eyes can just as easily see the nude in a naked figure as they can see the naked in a nude. It all depends on the heart behind the eyes. - *

A nude which has little if any affiliation with exhibitionism, which expresses warmth and confidence and an actual story, which has little or nothing to do with contemporary angst or submissiveness or abuse or domination, would best be described as a 'who' and not a 'which' or 'what.' Sad to say that such a wondrous nude is today rarely visible, or even recognized in the realm of the arts. - *

To know the difference between erotica and pornography you must first know the difference between naked and nude. - *

There is a lot to be said about the breast-heavy, female anorexic Barbie figures which make up our contemporary interest in bodies. And most of that should be expressed on a couch. - *

When you paint a nude in the nude, are you sure which one is the nude painting? - *

Reviewing the 1893 book: *Drawing the Figure for Children* by Caroline Hunt Rimmer, it seems obvious that it was once "normal" to present children with the reality of their bodies - that it was not a sin nor an aberration that children should know that one figure had a vagina, another a penis.

The same conclusion can be intimated when applied to the 1856 drawing of François Bonvin entitled "Boy Sketching" (Rather autobiographical if we know of the artist's childhood) in which a boy, approximately 9 or 10 is shown "normally" honing his skills by sketching a nude representation tacked to the wall before him. Today, our children seem to be taught at a very young age to fear bodies - theirs and everyone else's - to even fear what once attracted every child's healthy curiosity. How odd, in these purportedly enlightened times that we would consider it healthy to impose upon our children fear, guilt and ignorance - and all at the same time. - *

On Painting

If I paint a tomato, I am not trying to create a real tomato. I simply want to feel that delicious constricted reaction in my throat that fresh garden picked tomatoes cause. I want to taste it. Painting is a sensuous act, not an exercise in photo-copying. - 2013 *

To fall in love with France and Italy is to become enthralled with their every ochered shades, hues and tints. - 2013 *

Noonday sun, without shadows, is useless other than for being bored sitting on a beach. - 2010 *

How to paint convincing electrical wiring over architectural or natural surfaces in a landscape? Paint the sky, the walls, the trees; never paint the wires. . . Step back. If they need to be there, they will be there, otherwise they will have graciously and unceremoniously disappeared. - 2006 *

Complementaries and contrasts. Everything is about complementaries and contrasts - 2006 *

Painting is a series of alterations applied to an ever evolving perception. - 2001 *

Paint. Do it with determination. Fail if need be, but paint. Don't "try" to paint. Don't try to do your best. Do your best. Fail again? Recognize it and begin anew. That is what constitutes the everyday drudgery and wonder of a creative process. In the end, it is both exhausting and exhilarating. - 2001 *

It is not enough to know that receding planes will be cooler than non-receding planes. If they are. . . so be it; paint them that way. If they are not, for god's sake paint how you see them. If that doesn't work, just maybe you've learned something about your inability to see well enough to paint. - 1996 *

To the world, black may be the value of the darkest dark and white the value of the brightest light. To an artist, both black and white are equal and opposite voids between which the drama of life's full colours play themselves out. - 1994 *

When painting outdoors, the light falling on the subject is the same as on the canvas. And over and above setting this technical parameter, it also sets the mood. - 1987 *

What colour is white, if not a reflection of its nearest neighbour tinted by a warm or cool light. - *

The most wondrous painted walls are those which disappear when a painting or sculpture are placed before or upon them. - *

Loving or despising a subject has nothing to do with painting it, unless the goal is to paint a loved pretty or hated ugly picture. - *

The sharper the edge of a positive shape the more dramatic the separation of that shape from its juxtaposed negative space - *

Colour has no value if its only purpose is to be attractive. - *

Bristles are for every step in the painting process. Sables for last minute touches, for tweaking - or simply for ruining everything you accomplished before picking up the sable. - *

The test of a good painter is to use Indigo blue profusely. . . and successfully control it. - *

A bad painting remains a bad painting despite any and all lofty intentions, Masters diplomas or artistic statements thrown up in its defence. - *

A bad painting is one which is more often than not an exercise in self-absorption. And like a bad speech, it is endurable for the first five minutes. After ten, an enormous amount of patience and politeness is required to continue looking at it. After fifteen, it becomes unbearable, and after twenty minutes downright annoying for the repeated yawns it inevitably causes. - *

I become a good painter the day I stop rendering what is physically there in things and begin to render what is essential to that thing. - *

To successfully paint, focus on painting not on completing the painting. - *

A successful portrait is a drawing, a painting or a sculpture given life. - 2015 *

The most expensive paintings in the world are often portraits or artworks depicting the figure. - 2014 *

Back to the future. . . If contemporary painted portraits are to regain their classic status, the rendering of them must go beyond their consistently static poses, their obsessive flatness, their look and feel of badly copied snapshots.
Portraits must be given back their capacity to interpret "us" and to reach out beyond the navel of their creator - to connect and to speak with viewers. – 2014 *

Child portraiture revisited.

I was once "accused" of, amongst other things, painting only beautiful children. Such an insipid remark lacked dignity then and lacks it now - especially as it came from a journalist masquerading as an art critic.

To a painter, it is not a child's face which is beautiful. Rather it is the aura of the whole, through an alignment of perfectly proportioned elements which, combined, create a representation which elicits both a protectively emotional response and a sensual reaction. The same goes for adult portraits.

But there is something mysterious about child portraits. They always bring on more questions than answers. And in that more of them are masterpieces than traditional adult renditions.

A child portrait is not judged successful based on the proverbial "ooh-ahh" reactions a superficial physicality displays. Rather, excellence in its capacity to connect depends on the spiritual glow a portrait of a child emits - the aura of "possibilities" it represents. Even the portrait of a shy youngster must give a glimpse of that face's hidden array of endless spontaneous expressions; its incredible capacity to convey depths of feeling as well as calculated resistance to imposition.

Nonetheless, we cannot deny that it is through physical components well rendered that we connect to the "tangibility" of the face of a child - its large eyes powerfully scanning, analysing, discovering; the pug nose's twitching at aromas, smells and essences; ears hearing, listening, capturing, ignoring; mouth animated; mind completely enthralled with everything new, everything adventurous, everything truly "awesome".

And yet, it is at times the rather chilling calm and/or enigmatic contentment which reaches out to touch our ever so more tense adult selves. . .

More often than not, in a good child portrait, what is "real" is what shines through skin and sinew. This is in contrast to many adult portraits where, too often, we encounter a rather marketed or "acceptable" façade.

It is easier to find determination, concentration and empathy in a child's face well rendered. Why? Because, it represents a being not yet tainted by a need to dominate or control or to submit to the pressure of irrational fears, anxieties, worries or self-inflicted pains. Possibly that explains why our society is at times destabilized by a hate to love / love to hate ratio in our considerations of children. At times, they seem stronger than we are and this is rather disconcerting.

That being said, a successfully rendered portrait of a child is one which is founded on observation - on a connection with not only what they are but who. And oddly, when we take the time to observe such a subject, we inevitably discover ourselves. . .

It is then we realise that this child before us is possibly more than we were at their age - and in the future will possibly surpass our own self-anointed "incredibilities".

In essence, to assimilate information which professional observation affords us is to commit to the idea that, just maybe, we no longer are as powerful as this child is at that very moment in time.

Sketching out profundity demands we glimpse into the realm of a certain wisdom - like acknowledging the inevitability of our passing, through the simple discovery of "greater-ness" in a small package - one with a long and undefined life ahead of them.

All this to say, observation in the realm of portraiture is an exercise in sensual objectivity. Criticism nothing more than an ignorant subjective retort. Naturally, not everyone can (or should) paint child portraits. And, definitely, not every critic is learned whose shallow remarks pretend at cheekiness. - 2014 *

It takes a high level of skill to render likeness in a portrait and an even higher level of connectivity with others to render soul. - 2013
*

A hair well laid down is more important to the successful rendering of mood in a portrait than a profusion or intensity of colour.- 2013
*

When a portrait is revealed and we are told : "It really looks like him (or her)! That is a welcome compliment. But there is no recognition greater than hearing : "That's her!". "That's him!" - 2013 *

Lovers of people don't make better painters of people. Lovers of people are simply lovers of people. - 2013 *

A painter, looking at another, sketching another, painting the soul of another, within that rendition may not discover his own likeness; but might find himself. - 2013 *

A portrait which displays a high level of "likeness" celebrates a painter's technical skill - a subject's personality, a painter's ability to see, feel, project and communicate soul. - 2013 *

I recently received an email from an excessively angry person. I did not know her or had I ever met her. . . She wasn't angry at anyone in particular. She was just angry and in need of a scapegoat upon which she could lay down her wrath. I so wanted to see that aggressive face!
How wonderful it would have been to paint it, to just get to know the deep-down-inside menace controlling the muscle spasms of her venomous tongue, to paint the weight of that most probably

10.4

sneering furrowed brow.

Despite not having a webcam, I knew there were those eyes – eyes with a carefully honed piercing stare, whose only goal was to rip from me the smile I had worked on all day.

The challenge in portraiture is not so much the rendering of the petrified face but rather the capture of tone and mood and history – the present and future. . .

The focus in portraiture is on the ferreting out of every powerful emotion which lies hidden and pulsing and ready to spring forth - either to terrorize or gently caress.

In essence, what is more important than a smile or frown in a face is the secret fears, hates or love behind it. And that is the essence which makes a portrait a portrait. - 2012 *

The goal of a portrait painter is to make their subjects, whether adult or child, receptive to being "studied and rendered". And that can take a considerable amount of time, where contemporary children are concerned. So many of them have been taught early on to be wary, if not outright afraid, of anyone falling under the rubric of "stranger". And whether we like it or not, a portrait painter to most children is a stranger. - 2011 *

The study of a child's face is a serious undertaking. The intent is to dig deep enough in order to bring out "the person" from within that child. For the observer that can mean discovering a reflection of the best that we once were - but that we are no longer. And this may be more upsetting to the observer than to the observed. - 2011 *

If I am ever to look at myself in the mirror in the morning - every morning - I must be able to say unequivocally that everyone I have encountered has offered me a palette of who they are without my judging them beforehand. Without this standard, this rule of thumb, I cannot paint an honest portrait of anybody - not even of myself. - 2009 *

In 40 years I have never been given a portrait commission because I am of a certain colour, ethnic origin or of the right faith. But I have been refused a commission because I was not the "right gender", some because I did not have the "right ideology" and one because I was "straight" and therefore "couldn't be expected to understand or translate the right feeling".
Discriminating and being discriminated against in the field of portraiture is par for the course. You either live with it or get out of the field altogether. It's actually more a learning experience than a horror. - 2007*

A "try" at portraiture is nothing more than a good or bad physical representation of a body - unless, i.e., there is more to it than the rote connection of dots in a specific pattern - which just happens to visually say "physicality".
For a portrait to be a portrait it must dig deep into the life-blood of the physical. And, religious tenets aside, it must bring forth the soul - the beingness residing within which, for truth to be told, must over-ride the three-dimensional visual concoction of sinew and skin sitting before us. - 2005 *

The best way to achieve a portrait of the real child behind the "present" child is to be rid of the parents. - 2001 *

10.6

If I haven't captured the personality of a portrait subject, getting a likeness is meaningless. - 2000 *

As much as group portraits can be interesting, I prefer working with individual subjects. In them I become completely absorbed in the discovery of a personality, connecting, offering itself up. - 1998 *

Though many request their portrait painted, few truly wish it done. What they crave is to look like a photograph, but thinner. - 1997 - *

A portrait with neither likeness nor soul, isn't... - 1996 *

Seeing likeness in a portrait is to recognize the craftsman in the visual artist. Finding soul, is to discover the artist in the craftsman. - 1996 *

Most who are anxious to try their hand at portraiture should follow their initial instincts. . . Take two aspirin and forget it. - 1995 *

A portrait's breadth, its eyes, should make you shudder. - 1995 *

Everyone's hands are a picture of who they are. - 1995 *

A good portrait results in the meeting of two souls - that of the subject and that of the viewer. Once a painter has introduced the two, she should step back and intrude no more. - 1986 *

A painter of people prefers to pass unnoticed; to be left alone to notice. - 1986 *

10.7

A portrait varies. It is a thought, an emotion, a hint, a cry, a smile, a wince, a suffering, an enigma. The only constant is that a good portrait is always a question. - 1986 *

Being commissioned for an official portrait because we come from the same region as the subject to be painted is not a compliment - it's simply a standard reflection of proximity - a geo-political courtesy to first ask a kinsman to "do the work". For all intents and purposes, being chosen as the best for a job is the only good reason for getting it. - 1986 *

To successfully paint portraits I must recognize and sense the gentleness of one subject and the aggressive nature of another – yet remain separate from the emotional dictates of both. - *

A professional portrait painter or photographer may, in the process, discover himself in an evolving portrait. Yet, the viewer of a portrait should only be taken in by the wonders of the subject portrayed. - *

Eric Fischl - one of the bad boys of contemporary figurative painting - has carved for himself a niche in the portrait arena. Though faintly Lucian Freudish, the results are less portrait than they are enticements to have viewers be voyeurs, sitters be victims and the painter executioner. - *

You know a portrait commission is a lucrative "gig" when visual artists, who would never otherwise associate themselves with the lowly art of portrait painting, are the first to submit their names for the commission. - *

The status of portrait painters has always been suspect in the eyes of those who consider the genre a sub category of the lesser art of figure painting. Anti-portrait people "portray" this activity as "prostitutional", i.e.: one which earns you money in exchange for services rendered. . .

Ironically, such comments are attacks on those who have money in their pockets. . . the very problematic situation in which accusers would wish to find themselves.

But then, admitting to this would lose them the status of "whining struggling artist" which they have put so much effort into being seen to be. - *

The unique qualities of individuals often fade when represented in a group portrait. The overpowering presence of the most dominant person in the group tends to eclipse surrounding personalities - forcing them into subordinate supporting roles. - *

To recapture in contemporary portraiture that which Picasso sought, we must return to his teachings and rediscover his quest at the level at which we find ourselves - and that is usually far below where he was already by the age of 15.

In our haste to see portraiture as a way to flatter a subject or enhance our reputation as someone who can draw a good likeness, we fail to see that Picasso did see the value in this. But over and above that understanding, he gave more importance to the independent existence of that piece of work once he was through rendering it. - *

To paint a portrait is to present to the world the grandeur, the fallacy, the power, the weakness, the beauty, the ugliness, the incredible impossibility that we all are.

But to achieve this, to render it palatable, it is important to first leave our studio - to sit in parks and to walk about - and that for several years - before laying brush to canvas.

For the first year, it is important to will ourselves to see. If we are able to resist drawing during this time, so be it. If after having survived such a lenten period we still wish to, crave to, or passionately desire to begin to paint . . . then we will have assimilated enough observation and "seeing" to start rendering the human form as a viable network of communicable parts - and at our best create a mesmerizing whole.

For the next four years and more, the dictate remains : sketch, sketch and sketch even more. Once this feat has been achieved, we will most likely be appropriately trained in the art of "learning to paint essence". For only then, will we be able to adapt our "unique" observations to the art of rendering the human form at its most intimate and tactile. . . the portrait. - *

Critics of portraiture are often ignorant of the fact that all painters of the past, strived to become recognized working professionals. That a painter or sculptor would take the time and effort to apprentice, to practice, work and forge their way to a goal of self-sufficiency is a much older concept than the arts for art's sake mentality.

What contemporary visual artists fail to recognize is that professional artists have always been "laborers". They work for a living. They come from that batch of rebels who, like the Impressionists, learned their craft and honed their skills before they dared oppose the standard of the day.

Today, we consider rebellion a matter of course. Rebelling against what? Well, we haven't really considered that since we generally don't have the skills to offer better than our latest "teachers" have been giving us: i.e. : too much of the dipping of the brush into the crevices of our navels for inspiration and too little inspired expression.

All in all, portraiture is one of the few facets of the art world which has maintained its status as an unabashedly "working class" activity. - *

If we are interested in portraiture, but have not taken the time to analyze the hairs sprouting wildly from the ears of an old man or noticed the eyes of a child mysteriously changing when a smile is coming on or wondered at the scrawny bone protuberances of an anorexic's futile search for freedom beyond their greying skin, than you are not ready to paint "what is" or even less paint your expression of what, at times, is painfully known as reality.

Dignity recognized, in all forms of life, as well as the ability to transcend the obvious - that is what is required to convey the inner most soul of the subject of a portrait. It is the representation of the physicality of emotion rather than the emotion of physicality which differentiates between a fine copy of a person's body and soul and a simple pastiche which displays nothing more than a magazine pose. - *

When the body of a dead man still makes you cringe and the softness of a baby's bottom still makes you coo, it is understandable that viewers of your work would consider your efforts boringly ordinary and common. - *

10.11

People don't often get a chance to stare at each other - as painter and subject do. Sometimes a subject starts to feel like you can see inside them. And though they may shudder at the very thought of doing so, they unabashedly begin telling us about themselves. Posing is like being in a confessional. As a portrait painter I feel privileged to be considered worthy of the revelations I am at times offered. It's what makes painting the who and what of people a wondrous thing. - *

Contents of "Other World" Musings

On Children, Parenting And Mentoring

A child well loved is a loving child. - 2015 *

It must be fun being a kid today. . . Hovered over at home, spied on at school through *ClassDojo* (*an app that snitches on you real time to both your teachers and parents*). M-Hmmm. Get used to it kids. . . By the time you're an adult, freedom, self-expression and privacy will simply be antiques; giddy concepts spoken about in history lessons. - 2014 *

We have nothing more valuable to leave our children than the knowledge of how we faced and overcame adversity and failure and how elegantly we dealt with success. - 2014 *

To become "big", to control the environment which makes them sad, is the wishful thinking of discouraged children. - 2014 *

Caring adults don't plan the futures of their children and grand-children. They simply encourage their unfolding. - 2014 *

11.1

Increasingly, and this from an early age, we are "training" our children to not know freedom, to not be adventurous, to fear strangers and all other unknowns, to submit to an ever expanding array of safety rules and to accept from self-anointed specialists and authorities the politically correct blueprint for their "becoming normal" - i.e.: the same as everyone else. - 2014 *

Children are creatures of the present. They thrive on curiosity, discovery, creativity and awe. - 2014 *

Angry child? Fix the environment. Problem solved. - 2014 *

To say that a child has never had a childhood is to deny the legitimacy of the childhood that this child has had.
To say that a childhood can only be defined via acceptable social commonalities rather than individualities is to dictate that this child's chances of a mentally and emotionally healthy adulthood are limited.
Ironically, many unhealthy children, and eventually bland or "upset" adults, were "blessed" with a so-called "acceptable" normal childhood. - 2014 *

Children do not need to learn play skills - most especially from an adult. They need to be left alone to play. - 2013 *

To learn more than in our wildest dreams we ever thought we could, to be healthier in mind and body than we ever thought possible, we should observe a child playing for an hour each day - if we can find one playing freely without helicopter parents hovering. - 2013 *

A well designed playground is one in which parents (if they must be there) play their role from the sidelines – i.e.: looking appropriately worried, waiting for the inevitable fall and cringing at the very moments most children screech with joy. At best, playgrounds of merit are those which have been designed with no parents in mind. Let "them who insist" on overseeing play – (something about which they know nothing) – stand apart, wishing they were home. . . where they should be anyway. - 2013 *

*Limiter les enfants à l'enfance, les adolescents à l'adolescence, permet aux adultes de ne jamais leur ouvrir la porte à la vie adulte. - 2013 **

Self-reliance, independence and a sense of achievement in a child are only possible when parents stop being dependent on a child being dependent. - 2013 *

ADHD is a testicular disease which occurs when those responsible for the well being of children don't have the gonads to give them a life worthy of their station. - 2013 *

To most children the organized sport which comes closest to freedom and exhilaration is soccer. Nonetheless, it bears watching how long it will take for the controlling, schedule obsessed, need to win adult ways to eventually destroy that "game" too. - 2013 *

If during my childhood I am more titillated by licence than wondrous of freedom, I can no more, as an adult, have a conscience than experience shame. - 2011 *

Infants deprived of physical affection are crippled in their capacity to be loving. Similarly, children deprived of play are incapable of facing obstacles, of dealing with challenges, of making emotional connections or of growing up. - 2009 *

There is no greater discouragement then that felt by a child who is never given the freedom to wander, who is not encouraged to discover, to experience challenges or to savour the tingling feelings emitted by daring the unknown. And there is no greater depression than that of a child who must live through his parents' fears, regrets and discouragements. - 2007 *

"Le cri du jour. . ." - Several "bullying" comments

I deeply applaud any efforts to downsize the power of bullying and to advise children and adolescents of the dangers of such attitudes. But what has happened to us in the past does not, nor will it ever, define who we are. What we do with what's been handed to us determines a solid, or not, future - not bullying.
To be a victim is an experience, not a state of being as so many ill-guided organizations, specialists, governments and corporations are wont to make us believe.
In our effort to eradicate bullying from contemporary life, we must stop promoting the idea of victimhood. All it does is open the door to more bullying. Encouraging discouragement does nothing less than cement lifelong fears as normal and renders our children incapable of looking life in the eye. - *

Why is it that we do not spend the same amount of time and energy that we do on bullying focussing instead on dealing with the overall environment which promotes such behaviour? If our attitudes and statements don't change we will have to accept that we are being nothing less than cruel in the promotion of suffering. - *

11.4

Despite any and all hurts, we are responsible for teaching our children to get on with it, dare, be challenged by, stand up to life's inequities and move on - not cower in a corner because a bullying person or thing has succeeded in turning them into a permanent "jellowy-victim mass". - *

We must promote hope not be catalysts for despair. Discouraging our children from dealing with life is even worse than they being bullied. Why? Because the discouragement comes from those they love and trust. - *

Not so long ago, our childhoods were lived under established codes of a communal value system - one based on ethics and principles - on the concept that doing good was more powerful than being evil. Today, value systems are considered undue impositions on the egos and psyches of individuals - especially our sweet children. We no longer believe they should know failure or even "trying". They are given trophies for simply "being" and soon learn that whining and complaining achieve more than diligence and vision. And so, depleted of their capacity to survive, our children have come to live under a new system of rules of law - one formulated on fear - the fear of never seeing success as really possible and having to submit to more powerful environmental forces which will benevolently dictate what they in their anxious state should undertake or not. Instilling a code of submissiveness based on a life-style of retreat into puerile dependence and single-minded victimhood is psychologically and spiritually unacceptable . By doing so we are encouraging our children to evade what is real and to embrace the virtual - lest something "real" be demanded of them or frighten them off. In North America we are actually achieving the impossible : the creation of a clinging, limitless infancy tethered to life-denying ear-buds. - 2007 *

Being a good parent does not mean encouraging our children to be something. It means encouraging them to do something - and to cheer them on when difficulties arise. - 2007 *

As much as we consider the world a difficult and dangerous place for our children, what frightens them more is the fear in our eyes, the extreme weakness in our indulgent "yes", when an authoritative "no" would be a more honest response. - 2005 *

Ironically, educators have come to realize that "all" children are special and therefore have a right to a special education. But still so mesmerized by this extraordinary concept, no one seems to have considered implementing the discovery. . . - 2003 *

The childhoods we so often claim to have lost and missed are more often than not "myth'd". - 2002 *

When we see danger in everybody and everything, we instill fear in children. That, in turn, erodes their innate daring, curiosity and all manner of creative potential. - 2002 *

In our obsessive quest to eliminate failure and make every encounter and environment safe for children we are fast becoming the greatest danger to their mental and physical health. - 2001 *

Apart from being a sham slogan for every new child-oriented or educational fad, "child-centredness" is more a decorative adjunct to a self-centred adult world than anything related to better child-rearing perspectives. Foisting (abandoning?) adult responsibilities and privileges onto children and teens, under the guise of respect and equality, is immaturity at its worst. The most devastating in all

11.6

of this is that we actually believe the contemporary state of child-centred family life to be healthy and progressive. - 2001 *

Should we be proud of ourselves? We now live in an era where adult reactions to dastardly events cause more damage to children than the events themselves. - 2001 *

*Le harcèlement? L'intimidation? C'est ce que nous imposons à nos ados tous les jours. Comment-ce fait-il maintenant qu'on est tellement bafoué par les méfaits vers lesquels nous les avons poussés, et ça par l'entremise de nos manques d'encouragement et de notre rejet évident? - 2000 ***

Ah les experts. . . Lorsque le monde des ados est en crise, ils pensent pouvoir tout régler en ciblant l'agressivité "dite normale" à ce stage de leur vie. Si on était en vérité expert, on reconnaîtrait que les problèmes d'isolement et de rejet de "ce qui est" n'existeraient qu'au minimum - si de temps en temps, on donnait aux ados l'impression qu'on les aimait toujours. . .
Si les jeunes ne se sentaient pas aussi isolés, si rejetés des adultes, ils ne seraient pas aussi passivement agressifs. Ils ne seraient pas aussi virtuellement accrochés à tout ce qui leur permet de rejeter, à leur tour, ce stage adulte qui leur est refusé avec tellement de vengeance et d'appréhension par les 30 à 95 ans.
*Lorsque le réel n'est pas invitant, la mort spirituelle de la vie virtuelle attire, devenant de plus en plus sanglante et de moins en moins conscientisée; de plus en plus dominante des moeurs, des valeurs et des actions et réactions de base qui nous définissent humains. - 2000 ***

Discouragement is for children and old folks. - 1999 *

Loving parents guide their children through the minefields of life - all the while stifling the urge, and their fears, to completely smooth out the road before them. -1997 *

It is difficult to be a good parent when our own unmet childhood needs constantly subvert those of our children. - 1996 *

Child-centeredness has always been an iffy proposition. Its greatest flaw is that it presupposes that the adults administrating it are adult. - 1994 *

Hyperactive children are more disturbing than disturbed. - 1987 *

We all want to share in our child's life, as any valuable parent would. But kids prefer their parents to be parents. . . not chums. It's a serious mistake to not know the difference. - 1984 *

I have encountered more reality-based greatness in the hearts of eleven year old dreamers than ever there was in the hormonally abject antics of most 35+ year olds. - 1983 *

How we were taught to deal with situations as a child determines how we handle life as an adult. - 1983 *

You cannot expect a 9 year old to all of a sudden do as he is told when during all the previous years of his life he has been telling his parents and teachers what to do. - 1982 *

The ultimate family unit is a safe haven, allowing for the self-expression of each member whilst legitimately expecting the collaborative will of all. - 1977 *

If I never know what my mother or my father does, all the while I am squirrelled away at school, how am I to fully know myself? How am I to identify with those closest to me? How am I to recognize, appreciate and emulate - to feel connected? - 1977 *

Children are at the same time : the person we think they are, the person they think they are, the person they truly are, the person we want them to be and the persona they aspire to. - 1969 *

Children do not need us to solve all of their problems or over-protect them in times of difficulty. They need us in the wings - being watchful, supportive and encouraging. They need to feel that they are allowed to be curious and daring – to feel that we will not catch them at every fall but catch them when the fall is too great. - *

Growing up will become a more positive experience when children feel less grossed out by those who preceded them, and more edified and touched by what has been accomplished by them. - *

My whole childhood was spent being curious, analysing, dreaming, creating, sketching. I was often alone but never lonely.
Though the crime rate was significantly higher in the fifties, I was never afraid to be in any part of our tough industrial city. But then, I was never once taught to be afraid. I walked everywhere and nowhere for hours - blissfully discovering, observing and wondering - being sociable with strangers and yet preferring silence - to watch unwatched. That no one recognized I had been gone most of a day pleased me. (To a child, being invisible is at times a magical gift.)
Lacking in physical prowess and coordination, I practised sideline sportsmanship through admiration of those who could do what I couldn't. And despite being last chosen in playground activities

11.9

and suffering from chronic daydreaming in class, I survived. . . with nary a syndrome nor a multi-faceted deficit disorder applied to my child or adolescent being. Oddly, no one seemed perturbed by my being "different" - least of all, me.   By the age of 16, I was on my own - a stock clerk, living in a boarding house. . . blissfully ignorant of the world; being and becoming whatever it is we all seem to inevitably "begin to become" at one point in time.

And so, looking back - wondering as I often do. What would my life have been? And who and what would I be now? . . . if, like today's hovered-over children, I had been forced to live a more ordained and most euphemistically called "normal childhood"? - *

We've taught our contemporary adolescents that easy is better than being challenged and that our complaining about their "never doing anything" is what is normal. - *

Rejection felt by most adolescents is not so much from our neglect, our pushing them away, our sneering or negative attitudes. Rejection is more akin to our not bothering, not noticing, not smiling. - *

If being loved and cared for are in the balance, a child quickly senses when it is "necessary" to do innately cloying, bland and/or obviously non-sensical things. - *

We parents can be drunk, neurotic, psychotic, despicably sadistic or cruel. . . and still our children love us. No other emotional commitment comes near to such pure and total selflessness. How much we have to learn from those who merit, but rarely get, the level of respect that is their due. - *

11.10

"Helping professions" too often require family units to fit a predetermined homogenous model in order for them to more easily define "family" within a framework of statistical reliability and predetermined variables of "normalcy".

But since the beginning of time, societies have been plagued by those self-same variable inconsistencies - these anomalies best referred to as : individuals, creatives and eccentrics - those uncontrollable annoyances whose commitment and adherence to expectations have always been iffy at best. If anything, they are consistent in only two things : perturbing expectations and refusing to adhere to established order and "controllable" community structures. In essence, they are more disturbing than disturbed. - *

Despite their seeming naivete, 9 year old children of the fifties were far more street smart, far more capable of survival and adaptation than are most children, teens and young adults today. Today's youth culture and hovering anxious parents have made our children ultra-dependent, incapable of sizing up danger and unable to formulate their own uniqueness.

Children of the fifties were allowed exploration, adventure, and much free time away from adults. Today's children are smothered with attention, supervision, demands, prodding and controls. There is little if any room left for "being or becoming" anything.

A fifty's child would have gagged at the very concept of "quality time". Even children of the 19th century were more sophisticated survivors than ours. Though they had less than, they certainly had more wherewithal then. - *

Being an adolescent is difficult enough. But when you must compete for prime time attention with tripped out wanna-be 30 years olds and the made-over crowd of the 45 plus . . . it must be

11.11

down right annoying to be a contemporary teen. - *

On Environment and Society

The greatest lesson to be learned from the dignity and strengths of emigrant families is that once everything has been lost, there is no longer anything left to lose. And that is when hope rises once again in the hearts of new immigrants. - 2015 *

Democracies are not strong nor are they progressive because they allow their citizens to think or speak out. They are strong and progressive when their citizens have never once had to wonder or worry about whether they could or could not. - 2015 *

Societies need to feel realistically secure, not idealistically "safe". To that end, contemporary environments need more connected "beat" police walking our streets. . . connected to emergency wards, social agencies, churches, mosques and synagogues - and, yes, police headquarters - and this, at all hours of the day and night. A beat cop beats the aloof car cop connection any day. A constant presence, a constant familiarity, known faces. These are what citizens require to feel connected with, to feel the love for and to respect the men and women exercising policing services.

What contemporary societies definitely do not need is to be "physically" separate; walled away from those who are there to protect them. More police, robotically attired, riding about and hiding in their increasingly cold and ever-more overbearing and threatening armoured cars is what exacerbates contemporary policing problems, not solves them. - 2015 *

A democracy exponentially defined by its rules is decreasingly recognized for its freedoms. - 2014 *

*The parents of special needs kids work really hard to help their kids become independent. But society works really hard to make sure kids without special needs do not become independent. - (Lenore Skenazy) - 2013 **

Everything. . . including our democracies, has a best before date.- 2013 *

When we are asked how we "feel" rather than what we think - we are being asked to share emotions, gut reactions - not our thoughts, considerations, analyses or facts. And on such a foundation of communication and on the media aberrations we accept as newsworthy "productions", lie the fate of contemporary democracies. - 2013 *

Status quo is a state of being which sells safety and sameness as better than adventure and discovery. It encourages timidity rather than curiosity and creativity - which, by their very natures, question and upset the status quo. - 2013 *

The saddest thing which can be said about a culture is that it has none. - 2013*

When community values are in play, fewer rules are required to maintain cohesion and civility. But when a society abandons the essence of who and what it is, a door opens – a door to the abuses which inevitably occur when an excessive number of rules and laws are emotionally rather than logically adopted to compensate for societal apathy. - 2013 *

We should not expect the world to be a safe place. If it was, we and it would have died off long ago. To survive, we of the world, need an equal amount of danger counterbalanced by individual and collective intelligence and daring - a measured bravado tinted with warmth and caring for the wondrous folly of it all. -2013 *

Bullying, poverty, cruelty, abuse, racism, disingenuousness. . . All of these are byproducts of a soured environment. And no matter how determined we are to correct them individually, change is impossible unless a society, as a whole, focuses its attentions on the very environment within which these cancers emerge and grow. - 2013 *

Rules, regulations and laws formulated on a basis of fear, contaminate and eventually erode rational thought upon which all democratic principles, freedoms and creativity have been founded. - 2013 *

Societies once gathered in community, in empathy, to help find and reconnect a lost child. Today, crowds gather to self-righteously

12.3

berate parents for negligence; for having "allowed" a child to get lost in the first place. - 2013 *

Democracy is the most powerful and yet the most vulnerable socio-political structure ever designed by man. At its best, it is the greatest forum for individual creativity, innovation and growth. At its worst, it becomes too comfortable, too easy, too self-centred and too collectively weak to respect or stand up for itself.
A democracy, at this point, becomes vulnerable to take-overs - first and foremost by its most boorish internal elements who weaken it even more - thus preparing it well for an eventual extermination by outside forces. - 2012 *

We are environmentally handicapped by our own psychological needs gluttony. Never easily sated, we feed off of 24 hour a day news which convinces us crime and mayhem are rampant, when they are not. At the same time, 24 hour a day advertising convinces us life can be perfect "if only"- when, again, it cannot be.
No wonder our children tether themselves to an alternate reality - afraid of becoming us, who are virtually frozen, clinging to unrealistic expectations, hating what we see in the mirror and being frightened by what isn't there. Sad. . . The main catalyst for tech toys being used as soothers is collective depression. - 2012 *

The two main indicators of a society's overall health are : 1)- the degrees of freedom children of all ages exercise within a nurturing environment and 2)- the degrees of inclusion elders enjoy within a community.
If a hard look is taken at North American society, we see that children are rarely heard from or seen on city streets or parks at

any time during a given year. And after the age of 70 or so, elders rarely partake in communal activities other than those found in their "homes for the aged".

If these can be considered indicators, would it be reasonable to assume that the well-being of North America is rather precarious in the areas of both physical and mental health? - 2013 *

Bells ringing, children playing, men and women working and mentoring, our eldest elders shuffling about, discussing and reminiscing, people laughing, singing and arguing.

With even one of these environmental elements missing, there is no village, no town, no city, no mental and emotional oxygen – no life. - 2012 *

Bullying and Victimhood are born of and nurtured by the same environment. One cannot exist without the other. - 2012 *

The most abhorrent abusers of this victimhood era are those who treat it as a personal or commercial windfall. - 2007 *

Bullying is not an errant virus nor a separate flaw imposing itself upon the fabric of a society. It cannot and does not exist in a vacuum. As such, it is an integral part of the environment from which it stems and is nurtured. That it thrives in a context which fails to value individual worth over cloned sameness is obvious. But no regulations or laws can ever rid us of bullying.

No entity, whether government, school, charitable organization or family, can impose rules or guidelines which will eradicate abuse of any kind. For bullying to fade, to become less prevalent, a society needs have the capacity and willingness to recognize that it is a by-product of its own community health.

For all intents and purposes, to heal a society must incorporate (or if need be) reintroduce into its DNA that which has been lost: basic community standards and values.

Without them bullying, at all levels of society and in all age brackets, will do nothing but increase. - 2007 *

When the wisdom of the present is blinded by its own arrogant magnificence, only the reckless belligerence of youth is capable of saving us of from ourselves.

Had this not been an integral part of all human evolution, life as we know it would never have been possible, would never change. . . would never get better. - 2006 *

Marketing has sold us on the illusion of strength, The consumption of that illusion has made us weak. 2004 *

It is only through a striving, working hard society, one which looks onward and upward - not inward - that the finest forms of freedom of expression, of culture exist. - 2004 *

A democracy become too easy, become homogenous, requires ever increasing regulations, rules and laws to maintain the illusion of a semblance of "oneness". And this being so, the very essence of creativity, self expression and democracy cannot but erode. From within it is destroyed - not by some foreign threatening source - but by its own hand. - 2004 *

How amazing is it that "tolerance" (i.e. : to endure others) is viewed as a quality rather than the protectionist attitude that it is. Sadly, recognition, acceptance and appreciation of "the other in others" seems sorely lacking in our implementation of democratic principles and values. Tolerance is not a quality, it is a self-righteous attitude of superiority. 2002. - *

In North America we build things with a shelf-life. We build things to self-destruct, to fall apart. And yet, when they actually do, we are surprised. - 2000 *

The ability of a community to do battle with, to fend off threats of a physical, mental or emotional nature is proportionate to the relative strengths of its individual members.
No society is immune to threat or destruction when individual egos within that collective are in a weakened state. - 2000 *

Without entrenched belief systems and a set of strong universal values, all democracies fail. - 1996 *

*The means by which we live, have outdistanced the ends for which we live. Our scientific power, has outrun our spiritual power. We have guided missiles and misguided men. - (Martin Luther King, Jr) - 1963 *

A society which needs to feel good rather than think well courts extinction. - *

Through an aura of self-righteousness coupled with voyeurism the reality-TV ministry has legitimized bullying and the denigration of "others" - of those who are different - of those who are not "us". - *

To eliminate bullying, speaking on individual acts will never be enough. We must create an environment which feeds affection not alienation, respect not tolerance and real one on one communication and appreciation if not understanding.   What is most dangerous is that we seem to forget or ignore that bullying is not born in a vacuum. It is rooted in an environment which either accepts to feed or starve it.

Children are not born bullies nor do they acquire it naturally. They get it from the environment from which they stem and that is what is most frightening to them. - *

It is far easier to celebrate victims as heroes than deal with the problems which made them victims in the first place. - *

Emoting about bullies and bullying has more to do with sentimentality than it does logic or encouragement. - *

Though a cause may have integrity, rebellions are the realm of both heroes and obnoxious egos. Only through their actions are we able to determine which is which. - *

Revisionism is the art of obfuscation, of manipulation of reality. By denying or re-fabricating the context of an historical event, we are only arrogantly reconfiguring content to meet our present needs and expectations. - *

Cities need three things to survive as areas in which living is vibrant: "local" schools with no need for busing, faith centres and "piazzas" - i.e. : community gathering places "centred" in all local areas. - *

*Quoique individuellement accueillant, généreux et docile l'humain, collectivement, est souvent le plus scabreux des prédateurs. - **

Homogeneity requires sameness in the same measure that fear craves safety. - *

Most of what we consider to be abnormal behaviour is nothing more than a normal reaction to an abnormal situation or environment. - *

More often than not social activists are most evident in their quest to scream and impose views. . . and most noticeably absent once the achieved goals are in need of nurturing and maintenance. - *

12.10

On Excellence and Perfection

The only thing abnormal about failure is our inability to see it; to accept it as a normal part of the life cycle process. - 2015 *

Perfectionists are those who insist we all be as good as they pretend to be. - 2014 *

At the worst of times, politics arrogantly demands perfection of those who, in their less precipitous quest to encourage excellence, "get in the way" of the speedier proponents of perfectionism. - 2014 *

Today's best effort is the foundation upon which tomorrow's "better" is built. -2013 *

Unlike televised corporate advertising would have us believe, true success is neither growth nor a newer product but rather the never-ending pursuit of excellence. - 2013 *

Beware credentials and diplomas which are more expensively framed and more prominently displayed than the services being offered. - 2013 *

Reality TV teaches us to focus on our inner loser – not on our innate capacity to strive and do. It teaches us to emote rather than think, to berate and belittle ourselves and others. But mostly, it discourages us from daring to reach above and beyond being the best we can be. - 2012 *

When feelings of inadequacy encourage us to reach for the impossible goal that is perfection, it is most often then that we lower our standards; falsely enhancing our human performances by using anything which gives us the illusion of achieving excellence. - 2011 *

Success is not doing better than another but rather striving to do better than the best we achieved yesterday. - 2009 *

Perfection means blindly following imposed rules whereas searching for excellence encourages a modulation of perceptions and expectations, a reaching out beyond our basic knowledge and grasp of things. - 2007 *

To be awed by perfection is to be morbidly fixated on the end; on the ultimate that is death - the only solution to life's imperfections being unacceptable. - 2007 *

Why waste time and energy encouraging others in the pursuit of excellence when perfection is so easy to demand. - 2005 *

A perfect existence is one in which we all submissively do the same thing over and over again, in exactly the same acceptable way. Sounds a lot like having something no one really wants or needs. . . like the plague, maybe? - 2004 *

Excellence is never achievable when societies impose standards based on perfectionist dictates - or worse - evaluate and judge what is acceptable through a lowest common denominator lens of political correctness. - 2001 *

It is not that we are a stupid people but rather that, in fear of being discriminatory, we have come to accept and celebrate ignorance as learned thought and almost any banal achievement as genius. - 2001 *

Things going too well often get in the way of doing things well. - 1998 *

In our pefectionist need to weed-out the "errant blades" disrupting the comatose monotony of our perfect urban spaces, we must accept that we are much more lawn-care obsessives than ardent gardeners. - 1996 *

In our frenetic quest to attain perfection we have lost sight of excellence. - *

Excellence always recognizes past efforts, encourages present attempts and entices us to strive for tomorrow's better. Its goal? To reassure us of the ever present possible. - *

*Have no fear of perfection, you'll never achieve it. - (Dali) **

Perfection requires comparisons, judgmental evaluations and the imposition of only "acceptable" standards. Perfection, therefore, is never excellence. - *

Absolute truth is an absolute lie. - *

There is nothing like a naive question emanating from the ranks of amateurs to upset the absolutist diatribe of self-appointed specialists. - *

13.3

How to parent, how to teach, how to play, how to work, how to raise children, how to do it, how to gauge it, how to analyse it, how to end it. . .

Life's lesson plans are no longer passed down from generation to generation. In our flustered era, we've outsourced the teaching of common sense to self-anointed specialists who have none to offer. - *

Absolutes are more easily dismissed than absolutists. - *

On Freedom and Fear

Security and safety must never be mistaken one for the other. The former is an intelligent construct allowing an established and functional environment to protect its hard won freedoms, values and culture. The latter is nothing more than a social control mechanism whose sole purpose is to induce fear and an ensuing societal paralysis. - 2015 *

Despite our purported evolution, we are still most frightened by and are most afraid of the one thing that once caused the most anxiety, the most fear in cave dwellers - each other. - 2015 *

The only friend of extremism is extremism. Freedom of determination is its most and only powerful enemy. - 2015 *

By restricting freedom "in the name of freedom", we give birth to a burgeoning acceptance of submission. . . again, in the name of freedom.. - 2015 *

Freedom means being free of fear, not free of responsibility or determination. - 2015 *

Fear, the designated kind, the politically recognized "it is time to be afraid" kind, the extremist caused and retaliatory promoted kind is what we should fear most - not terrorists or terrorism. - 2015 *

Bullying, by any means or "imposer", is impossible if no one accepts to be a victim. - 2015 *

Submitting to fear, changing who we are to meet a "new and improved" imposed standard, when who and what we were before an attack was "just fine", is to cow-tow to extremists from both sides of the proverbial coin. - 2015 *

In the end, will the 21st century be defined as one in which we have feared more than we have embraced, hated more than we have loved? - 2014 *

The more we are offered protection, the more we become dependent – victims – less curious, less daring, less wondering, less questioning, less able to think, analyse or fend for ourselves. - 2013 *

Freedom, cloaked in a mantle of fear, is nothing more than an illusion. - 2013 *

A truly free nation is one whose greatest focus is on education and the arts, not policing and military pursuits. - 2013 *

Security can only be found in facing the fears we have and in knowing the difference between those who inform us of fears being imposed and those who benevolently impose them upon us. - 2012 *

How odd that journalists travel the world to speak out on foreign government irregularities but are more than reluctant, if not afraid, to speak out in their own homelands. - 2011 *

The purpose of instilling fear, is to ensure that anxiety imprints itself upon the collective minds of those who we wish to convince are in need of someone to keep them "safe". - 2011 *

What contemporary fears have done to us all, as individuals and as nations, is almost impossible to fathom. - 2005 *

The silence of those who are free is the terrorist most feared by those who are not. - 1997 *

To be truly alive, is to create, to judge no one, to live judiciously and to be free of domination. - 1992 *

Ignorance does not create anxiety. The belief that we are fools, because we are ignorant, does. - *

There will always be those who will do anything to keep us frightened. Our best response is to be ever more unwavering, ever more determined, ever more brave. - *

Twenty-four hours a day, news blares, blasts, lures – forever repeating itself, convincing us to watch for more updates, further details, more reasons to worry, to be constantly fearful - and in between each segment. . . these awesome products being promoted to make us feel better.

And so, before our consuming world's never-ending crises, there is nothing left but unfathomable feelings of helplessness eerily coupled with soothing new and improved products which we cannot do without.

Is it then surprising that there is no time or inclination for us to think, to measure, to weigh. . . to be logical or strong minded. - *

The most vital of communities exists only when and where there is a balance between security and freedom of expression. - *

In order to exist and thrive, censorship requires that another's thoughts and considerations cannot. - *

14.4

On God and Good

Choosing to do things well, honestly, correctly is not the same as being imposed upon to do so. - 2015 *

Righteousness is collectively generous - celebrating the goodness within - despite the flaws in all of us.
Self-righteousness is personal. It negates goodness in others by highlighting the flaws within and finding pleasure in crushing the totality that we are.
Righteousness is objectively just while self-righteousness feeds on subjective cruelty.
Righteousness leads us to God where self-righteousness leads to vengeance, witch hunts and inquisitions. - 2014 *

The greatest difficulty today is distinguishing those who use God's name in vain from those who use it to spread love and harmony. The modus operandi may appear to be the same, but the goals are dangerously different. - 2014 *

15.1

The self-righteous see sins as an affront to them rather than to God. - 2014 *

A truth to be truth, must be more factual than authoritative. - 2014 *

History constantly reminds us that moralists are far more often associated with amorality and immorality than morality. Proselytisers amongst us are many, saints rather few. - 2013 *

When we all start believing we are the only ones right. It isn't long before there is no one left to be right. - 2013 *

Evil often disguises itself as the face of good and when truly evil the face of God - 2013 *

When morally right becomes "I am what is right and good" political, factual, social, scientific and authoritative truth fades. - 2013 *

Who should we most fear? Sinners? Or those who seem to spend more time thinking about sins than those they have determined are sinners? – 2012 *

Judgements based on a rigid thesis of black and white are always extremist. Founded on self-righteousness and the arrogance of power, they negate the multiple shades of grey within which God "dipped all of us" in His quest that equality, honesty and justice be well served. - 2011 *

Truth is never anything else but truth. It is neither mine nor anyone else's. Unbiased, it is independent of manipulation, power, greed, envy, vengeance, manipulation, love, propaganda or hatred. It is despite us all, simply and universally, truth. - 2003 *

An absolutist is much more interested in being seen to be absolutely right then in speaking the absolute truth. - 1998 *

Without the "mind's eye", truth becomes absolute, facts infallible, creativity impossible, innovation obsolete, discovery implausible and stagnation inevitable. - 1997 *

Pure vision is more in need of an open mind than a perfect soul. - 1993 *

The inalienable powers of abiding faith often anger and render jealous those incapable of expressing themselves other than through religiosity. - *

Remembering little and forgetting a lot has one distinct advantage - a less bitter lifestyle. - *

God is happy when we are happy, sad when we are sad and most disgusted when we waste the precious life given to us sucking our thumbs for hours on end. - *

Depuis le début des temps, aucun des grands dieux n'a commandé à ses disciples de tuer. Depuis le début des temps, ils nous ont encouragés à attirer, d'aimer. Ce ne sont que les voulant être dieux qui commandent hypocritement les tueries aux noms des

15.3

*dieux. Les aimants, les vrais aimants des dieux, comme Dieu, embrassent. - ***

Some amongst the reborn are not annoying because they believe what we infidels fail to grasp but rather because they live too publicly their own reactions to having had a "past life". . . never truly comprehending the desperation which demanded they be reborn and mostly the fear that, just maybe, they are "really" not. - *

How loud and obnoxious and arrogant are the self-righteous demands of those who would impose. How respectfully silent, contemplative and content the true believer in his quest to quench the thirst of those in need. - *

Those who would most wish to improve the world are often those who fail to look in the mirror. - *

Apologizing for the sins of our forefathers is not only naïve and the worst kind of political correctness it is also the one action which minimizes their sins, their goodness, their failings, their accomplishments - their lives.
By taking on a guilt they possibly never experienced we render their actions benign, their lives irrelevant to the unfolding of time. Apologizing for another belittles and even whitewashes perpetrations and responsibility. In essence, it is a feeble attempt at revisionism and the one act which surreptitiously begins the process of "forgetting".
The only way past sins can be atoned for is to remember that they existed, to remember the effects they have had and continue to have on others and to always remember that these negatives were

15.4

committed in the past by those we should never forget - lest we repeat what they did or what was done to them. - *

Truth is a wondrous, humble thing which can never be imposed. It is most persuasive and respected at its simplest and least trusted when enthusiastically sugar-coated, exaggerated, manipulatively emphatic or dominant. - *

Truth is emotionless as it is a statement of fact which belongs to or stems from no one or no thing. It simply is. - *

15.6

On Knowledge and Wisdom

Different people know different things and on that the world revolves and evolves.

But whether we are of the learned or the learning, it is important to fathom the difference between information offered by those who wish us knowledgeable and that imposed by those who wish us ignorant. - 2015 *

To ask a question is not a display of ignorance. Rather, it is a sign of intelligence. That's why, when we do, it frightens those who would rather we stay ignorant. - 2015 *

To those who exploit knowledge, it becomes an unrelenting ally. To those who choose ignorance as a companion, knowledge is an ever present threat. - 2014 *

Today's media tends to dismiss facts and thinking, focussing more on superficial reactions at a time when feelings have come to mean nothing more than emoting. - 2014 *

Going to school does not make us bright. It makes us learned. What we do, after school, with what we have learned, proves us bright. . . or not. - 2014 *

A diploma recognizes that a student has completed with satisfaction all of the courses required to obtain the title of "graduate". As such, the acquisition of a diploma is not a major achievement but rather a major "step" towards the realisation of a targeted goal. For all intents and purposes, acquiring a diploma opens the door to an opportunity to match our purported abilities with our actual successes in learning.

A diploma, therefore, is a "permission" to move on from the academic arena to that of apprenticeship, to that of application. Being "diploma'd" we can begin proving to seasoned professionals and to the world at large that we can "do it".

For all intents and purposes, until an approved level of competence and achievement is arrived at, the title on the diploma remains solely the title of the diploma. - 2013 *

Wisdom comes peacefully, not aggressively, speaks softly, not angrily and creates daringly, not submissively. - 2007 *

Answers which have a finality about them - which refuse to go anywhere beyond where they are - irritate. Questions, on the other hand, invigorate. Life opens up when a question is asked. - 2003 *

The measure of true intelligence has much less to do with having the right answer and much more to do with knowing how to and from whom we can obtain it. - 2000 *

It is an illusion that we are better informed than in the past. A heavier dose of digitally acquired lowest common denominator stimulation does not constitute a more informed mind, a more substantive thought, a more caring viewpoint. It simply makes what we now know more palatable. . . more politically correct, more "user friendly". - 1999 *

Pure vision is more in need of an open mind than a perfect soul. - 1993 *

If our hunger is to correct rather than learn from the errors of the past, we will one day encounter but never recognize, the avoidance of reality we practice today. - 1993 *

Contrary to popular belief, a democracy dependent solely on collective thinking, can only coast. To survive and thrive, whether locally, regionally, nationally or internationally, it needs individuals considering, wondering and thinking beyond the obvious. To that effect, elemental philosophy should be on the curriculum of all the grade schools, from grade 3 onward. - *

Digital tablets offer no more depth of learning than that which was available when the dust of chalk filled classroom air. - *

*The illiterate of the 21ˢᵗ century will not be those who cannot read or write but rather those who cannot learn, unlearn and relearn. - (Alvin Toffler) **

The human race is the only species which seeks knowledge to not only fortify its own existence, actions and survival but to also

16.3

avoid all responsibility for the destruction it leaves in its wake. - *

What arrogance ignorance often displays - *

On Life and Love

Love is what we feel when we miss someone dearly and, from afar, their skin tingles with the anticipation of coming home. - 2015 *

Life at its most healthy, teaches us to be vigilant, not afraid. It is when we take it for granted that it becomes unhealthy; that we become fearful, submissive, apathetic. - 2015 *

Life, at its best, is a wondrous process. Otherwise it is nothing more than an overly emphasized and superficially celebrated end run. - 2014 *

Dying is only democratic in so much as we all go through it at one point in time. Otherwise it's quite fascist. We, more often than not, have no choice in the matter. - 2014 *

Nearly 60 years ago, researchers H. Harlow and L. Rosenblum, discovered that children who failed to be touched, held and hugged from infancy onward, showed signs of abnormal brain development, of being disturbed, and of potentially developing violent tendencies.

Rather than embrace the obvious, we in the 21st century have become even more touch and body phobic than we ever were in the 50s. So busy are we with our own "self-esteem" issues, we've invented high 5s and fist bumps to increasingly replace the too tactile (too sensual?) hugs our children crave. - 2013 *

The late 20th and early 21st centuries have been in a love hate relationship with physical affection - with bodies. And so, we've invented a Harlow style surrogate. . . a mechanical toy that hugs unconditionally - on call. . . Welcome to our weird world Big Hugs Elmo. - 2013 *

Life is not perfect, neither is it completely safe nor ever will it be. But most of all, life is not a penance for our original sins as would have it those who are obsessed with finding (within us) life's every flaw (and if there isn't one to be found) create it. – 2006 *

*L'amour se nourrit de présences et d'absences, d'actions et de silences, de paroles et de désirs, de constances et d'aventures, de soirées calmes au sein d'un nid comme des voyages planifiés ou imprévus. Venise nous rappelle tout ça et plus. - 2003 **

Sad are those who have no concept of passion. Sadder still those whose perception of it is nothing more than the exaggerated emoting of obsessions. There's is a world of illusions. - 2003 *

A well managed life is efficient. A well lived life rarely is. - 2000 *

We are all smart enough to get at least one thing out of life. Wanting it all inevitably gets us nothing. - 1990 *

Life is neither incredibly wonderful nor incredibly horrible. More often than not it is simply horribly and wonderfully incredible - 1981 *

*J'ai horreur de la mort donc je suis ivre de vivre - (Jacques Sternberg) **

Life is all about ignoring the past's boastings, cherishing the present's heartbeat, and anticipating with awe the miraculous unfolding of the future. - *

Love can never be defined by those who cannot love - by those incapable of feeling the intensity of a look returned, the caress of a finger tip, the brushing of a lock of hair, the thought of another, the shiver of memory, of enjoyed time, of shared waking and deep sleep holding on. - *

The oversimplification of life's processes inevitably renders the mind simple. - *

Jealousy, despite its acceptance as a normal human emotion, is nothing less than an intense and often dangerous insecurity expressed in an accusatory fashion. Rather than based on the jealous one's perceptions of themselves, jealousy is more a reflection of how they feel the world is negatively relating to them and not how they actually relate to the world. - *

Since love is beyond space and time, existing beyond even the beingness of those who are in love, who and what we love can never be determined, defined or confined by the conventions of

17.3

those whose need it is to regulate it. - *

To understand a child is to know the very essence of life and love. To be an adult is to generally have forgotten all of this. - *

When infidelity is considered simply something which "happens", it is not surprising that jealousy is considered a normal element of love. - *

Jealousy is nothing less than a psychologically violent control mechanism and an inability to accept that in reality we are not the completely lovable entity we believe ourselves to be. - *

Love is looking at someone we have looked at a million times, and still we smile. - *

On Observation

It is only with both feet planted firmly on the ground, that soaring with dreams is not an illusion. – 2013 *

Hockey will regain the respect it deserves the day we appreciate excellence of play more than we are titillated by bullies and goons. – 2011 *

Validity and vapidity are more closely related than in their number of syllables and sounds. Without a process imbued with the former, the end result of any enterprise is nothing more than the latter. - 2004 *

Depression is to fall into a deep sleep and to no longer want to awaken; to do what once we did lovingly. - 2001 *

Success is when our work is more easily recognized than we are. - 2000 *

On est trop souvent aveugle devant les merveilles de l'ordinaire. - *

18.1

When everything is awesome, nothing is. - *

A consumer is not a collector anymore than a tourist is a traveller. Consumers "consume". They passively gorge themselves at the all you can eat buffet table of blandness; taking in the most they can. A collector, on the other hand is a passionate gourmet who may have funds for only one good painting or an exquisite antipasto. But if that is all they can allow themselves to "have", they savour every aspect or morsel of it. *

So many of us will do almost anything to experience visual nirvana. And so, we fly off to exotic places where nothing is familiar, everything exotic. We take in novelty as an hors d'oeuvre, capturing what is out-of-the-ordinary, domesticating it, making it daily fare.
Travelling is a delicious and creative adventure. And yet, all of it is often simply a prelude to an even greater feast - the discovery of our own backyard as primary source of inspiration. Apart from expanding our horizons, that is what travelling is for - to bring us closer to home. - *

Some say more in whispers than others wildly ranting and screaming. - *

For as long as we are more fascinated by the tools we use to communicate than the poetry of our statements, we will say and share nothing. - *

Before talent, before technique. . . relevance. Without relevance there is nothing. - *

To observe is to see beyond looking. - *

18.2

Upon hearing : "We've enjoyed having you?" What does one reasonably respond? "Hope you enjoyed being had?" - (Claude Poulin, English professor, incredible wit) *

For silence to be warm it must have the rhythmic cadence of a heartbeat, the soothing texture of a wave-washed beach, the sensual treble of a windblown kiss. For the richness of silence lies in its soft embrace and its patient acceptance of it constantly being broken by those who need noise to feel alive. - *

Self-expression is for babies and seals, where it can be charming. A writer's business is to affect the reader. – Vincent McHugh (1904-1983) *

Observation is an exhilarating exercise. Making time stand still for the observer; allowing for a wondrous mood to take over, forming a base upon which a powerful analysis of what attracts us can be built.

At its most exciting, it reveals the personality of an individual, place or thing - with the essence of the observed simply radiating; touching the lives of others in such a way as to better them without ever exuding an iota of superiority.

At other times, observation can be frightening - unwittingly unveiling the darkness behind a mask, the aura of a secret malevolence which may not even be recognized by the observed as actually being transmitted. - *

A loving and generous gift ill received is no less loving and generous. - *

The difference between observation and staring is in how we see what we are looking at. When we look at others do we see the smile or the bad teeth, the wrinkles or the gentle touch, the big nose or the Romanesque quality of a facial feature?

If our perception of the world is based on how we think the world should be, rather than on the recognition and appreciation of what is, we should never pick up a pencil to sketch, a brush to paint, a camera to shoot or a pen to write. - *

Observation is not and must never be a control mechanism. It is a tool of non-judgmental analysis which, once it becomes a honed skill, permits the viewer a glimpse of what truly is rather than what we wish a subject be, believe it to be or want it to be. - *

Hope exists, even if we cannot see it. - (Dominic Bercier, visual artist, spiritual story-teller). *

The value of words is more easily recognized once the power of silence is appreciated. - *

Our era is a world of confusing juxtapositions and revisionist associations where words no longer evolve but are rather appropriated. . . Today, we ironically read :

change as progress

charm as authenticity

common sense as naïveté

compensation as satisfaction

demands as rights

existing as living

growth as progress

homogenization as globalization

insult as honesty

infatuation as love

invasion as liberation

kitsch as creative

obsession as passion

overprotection as love

licence as freedom

perfection as excellence

nude as naked

revisionism as history

discipline as abuse

narcissism as ego

pornography as erotica

criticism as critiquing

tolerance as respect

opinion as fact

victim as hero

ruling as leading - *

18.5

18.6

On Power and Authority

We are the power behind elected officials. And the sooner we remember that, the sooner they will remember to lead rather than rule. - 2015 *

The most abused phrase by the self-righteous is always: "It's the right thing to do." - 2014 *

Contemporary principles are fast becoming fundamentally rigid; our capacity to appreciate differences and to respect others deficient to the point of reality TV schadenfreude - which, in real life, borders on evil. - 2014 *

Crashing in real politics is more about being poorly advised than performing poorly. - 2014 *

Too many politicians surround themselves with political advisors who know nothing other than politics. The collective expertise needed to get a politician elected is never the same as that required to maintain that person's position, once he or she has achieved the electoral goal.

To assure longevity, a politician must spend more time, from the very beginning, amassing a credible cadre of expert and wise advisors within the wide community of the electorate. - 2014 *

When authorities promote the idea of making us "safe", what they actually mean is : victimized and submissive - not freer, more engaged or more secure. - 2013 *

There is a universal savagery in contemporary politics which is increasingly reflective of the gradual disintegration of the world's democratic principles and ideals. - 2012 *

That we espouse self-esteem over self-respect is a mirror reflection of the narcissism increasingly dominating our decision-making processes. - 2011 *

Reaction is the child of "tweets" and texting and a "victim vs criminal element" mentality. It is emotive and defeatist and therefore subjective. Though more swift, it serves only the needs of reactors.

Action, on the other hand, plods along slowly - the servant of thought, analysis, and the creation of objective solutions. And in the end, it serves the needs of all. - 2013 *

Over-reacting is what authorities too often do when an event occurs before which they should have taken proactive steps. - 2013 *

Our societies are desperately in need of intelligent policing, not more police intelligence. - 2012 *

19.2

No country is ever immune from being hijacked. And as with most abuse, it is usually perpetrated by those we already know. - 2012
*

*In the process of making a god of our leader, we have made sheep of ourselves. - Quote by Dalton Camp (1920 2002) in regards to the exaggerated reverence paid Diefenbacher. - **

For all intents and purposes, census provides a population with factual determinants which analyse the needs of and the required services to be offered a country's varied elements. The first step in the censorship of census, therefore, begins with the elimination of information deemed not acceptable by those who would rule rather than lead. And this is why census is one of the first services which must be curtailed if a democracy that we know is to ever become the autocracy our children will acquire.

The less a country knows about itself, the less it has the capacity to obstruct its own demise. Ignorance, therefore, is the bliss of the unfree and the necessary tool of those who would control. One can only govern with impunity through ignorance. And the elimination of a true census - i.e. : elimination of the facts about a country's functions and peoples is the groundwork upon which national ignorance can be formally instituted under the guise of protecting individual and collective "privacy".

With individual and collective traits thus denied identification, a national forum, built upon the sameness of homogeneity, can more easily be implemented and institutionalized. And this acceptance of a completely blended nation shall then be promoted as being the foundation of nothing less than a benevolent and patriotic realm of peace and tranquillity.

In essence, difference is dangerous to those who would eliminate the recognition of it through census. Differences have a tendency to resist control. And this is so in such an intense way that difference - its recognition and appreciation - is the only thing which protects us from actions which would lead to total domination.

When we are no longer aware of or are made to feel uncomfortable with the wondrousness of difference, all we will come to know is sameness, homogeneity and the fear of that which once fascinated us. Through ignorance, the idea of difference being dangerous is born - not because difference threatens but rather because we are advised that it is a threat.

The very concept of census is to allow a population to not forget that its diverse elements are the riches of its collectivity - not the causes of its failings. Without a full census, we begin to forget, to un-know, to not think, to be ignorant of anything other than that which we are told is true and thus is born the very cause of a democracy's eventual demise : "political correctness" - 2011 *

An excellent politician is one who listens. A good one pretends to listen and gets away with it. A bad politician pretends to listen while obviously looking over our shoulder - in search of someone else more important to speak with. - 2005

It is not the right or left of things which is dangerous but rather the extremes of both which feed on our lowest common denominator basal instincts and fears. - 2005*

We have been coerced into believing that as long as we are "open", that we talk about what ails us, problems eventually get solved. Actually, this bullshit illusion too often masks truth. The more we are scripted to "talk out our feelings" the more we are taught to feel about and the less we are taught to "think and do" about our problems. - 2003

It is not the philosophy nor the creed which should make one shudder but rather the degree of fanaticism with which a premise is promoted or imposed - 2001 *

If experts spent as much time actually working on and improving relationships between races, religions, men and women, children and adults, employees and employers, as they do obsessing about how we "should" deal with things, just maybe progress would be possible. - 2000 *

When we are so intimately linked to the lives of others that ours becomes nothing more than a blur, we are either a too long in the field member of one of the helping professions or we are in need of one of them. - 2000 *

Those who feel the need to endlessly emphasize that abuse is a daily occurrence, do so in order to avoid doing what actually needs doing in order to improve the environment which nurtures such abuse.- 2000 *

Modern helping professions are too busy imposing "normalization" on all of us to notice that their approach to life is one of human stagnation: i.e.: that which destroys passion while nurturing obsessive sameness. - 1998 *

19.5

A controlling ego should never be mistaken for a strong one. – 1998 *

The most dangerous societal structure is the one which is built on a democracy which removes authority and responsibility from the hands of elected officials and places it in those of its bureaucracy. - 1998 *

Our predatory need to bring down those we consider the "elite" (in order that we feel elevated) most often accompanies an additional unhealthy need to gloat as they lie at our feet. - 1996 *

Radicalism's self-interest is more attuned to screaming the loudest than actually achieving positive change. - 1996 *

As long as a finger is pointed at the problem, the cause slinks by unnoticed. - 1996 *

Politicians at the end of their careers generally fit into one of three categories : those who did it to the people, those who did for the people and those who were one with the people. - 1996 *

The success of today's political systems eerily seem dependent on their ability to maintain the middle class in a state of contented intoxication and the perceived lower classes in a state of benign agitation. - 1995 *

*You can't confuse political passion with political ambition. - (B.Streisand) **

Power maintains. . . Influence changes. - *

Ours is an era of emotional reaction, not considered action. Under such circumstances, solutions being proffered are more often than not wrong. - *

Through the internet, corporations and countries, which once saw themselves as huge, powerful and invincible, now discover themselves to be rather small and insignificant in the grand scheme of things. Underestimated, the growing power of the internet has fallen into the hands of "the people". And as a result, those who would see themselves as our overseers have become anxious; hell bent on taking back control of that dastardly democratic accessory. - *

Those who would most wish the world improved are often the same who fail to look in the mirror. - *

Democracy's "will of the people" is too often defined by those who foist their opinions upon those who fear voicing theirs. - *

Contemporary democracy fails us all when it accepts that power and academic qualifications are more valuable than the wisdom of elders and the authority of the competent and experienced. - *

There is nothing more insulting to a citizenry than to discover that it is considered nothing more than a gaggle of subordinates and victims by those they have elected to office. - *

A bureaucracy is only as sadistic as its citizenry is masochistic. - *

19.7

19.8

On Science

The latest revision of the *Diagnostic and Statistical Manual of Mental Disorders* (DSM-5) is the most pharmaceutically influenced manual of its kind ever. It gives credence to the notion that humans, in their uncontrollable diversity, are considered to be nothing more than wild wheat germ in need of a genetic modification "fix". . . - 2013 *

Neutering difference is akin to the elimination of creativity - to a mass cloning of individuals, to eventually rendering humanity docile, silent and subservient. - 2013 *

Walking is universally known to be one of the best treatments for depression. Then, why are its benefits not promoted by doctors far and wide? Because pharmaceutical entities cannot profit from a walking regimen. Worse. . . It has side-effects. It's addictive. - 2013 *

As long as comic strips say more truths about us than a $100 plus an hour analyst, newspapers will remain a good buy. - 2012 *

Espousing profits rather than pure science, contemporary corporate research too readily allows for a myriad of "acceptable" result categories befitting more the secondary effect realm of maybes, shoulds, coulds, mights, and possiblys than the reassurance arena of definitives. - 2012 *

On Self

Contemporary perceptions are filled with too much Hollywood emoting; not enough legitimate human emotion, too much licence; not enough freedom, too many rules; not enough self- discipline. - 2015 *

Choice is not a matter of submitting, cringing or whining. It is, as implied, a matter of "choosing"; of deciding what is and getting on with doing what needs doing. - 2014 *

If I travel to Italy (or anywhere else in the world) it is certainly not to share how "selfie-wondrous", how grandiosely insipid I am in a Florentine, Roman , Grecian or Peruvian monument kind of way. It is to discover, beyond our "selves", how wondrously different and yet the same the rest of the world's people and places are. - 2014 *

If the narcissistic concept of "self-esteem" had any validity it would have long ago matured into self-respect. - 2014 *

The self more obsessively becomes the object of our fascination and angst during those periods in our lives when all is too boringly comfortable and tranquil to be of any value to the success of our evolving. - 2014 *

Women see children as beings becoming, men as beings resembling themselves. - 2013 *

When we feel angrily entitled, put upon, excluded, saddened; when we have yet to find ourselves and are upset because we do not have what we want out of life. . .
When at the slightest of provocations we crave a self-esteem fix - as we are taught to do by those who profit from our fears and whining. . .
When we are down and depressed about the least little thing, we should think "Malala" and be ashamed that we are such a sad example of God's greatest creation. - 2013 *

How interesting that when we are silent we are accused of keeping secrets. . . And when speaking enthusiastically, of masking truth. To others, at times, we will never be enough or will always be too much. It is only within ourselves that contentment is at all possible. - 2013 *

Handwriting is to identity what typing on a keyboard is to invisibility. - 2013 *

In past centuries, those who espoused the supercilious mantras of "I am beautiful" and "I am special" had the common courtesy of keeping the focus of their affectations to themselves. - 2013 *

21.2

The Oxford Dictionary announces "selfie" word of the year. With the 21st century fast becoming the most self-centred era of all time, could a more accurate choice have been made? - 2013 *

There is no more vacuous statement we can teach our children than: "I am beautiful". - 2013 *

I am a 21st century male. . . Therefore suspect. . . - 2013 *

Without others we are not. - 2013 *

*Dans le domaine des arts, il faut savoir disparaître pour permettre à la créativité d'apparaître. - 2013 **

I am the least of my curiosities because, of all of my interests, I am the most boring. - 2013 *

Men who feel gonadectomized by women of stature and prominence are generally those who have the least to lose. - 2013*

Contemporary self-esteem is to mirrors, entitlement and narcissism as self-respect is to reaching out, to discovering a world beyond the self - a world called "others". - 2012 *

*Lorsqu'on persiste à regarder par en arrière, à fuire les spectres du passé, on manque souvent de noter les embuches devant nous. . . et aussi les fleurs. - 2011 **

We are born innocent. And from that time foreword, never more. - 2010 *

21.3

As long as we see evil in our bodies, as long as we see our physical selves as a threat, as long as our very existence is equated with sin - is how long we will be a frighteningly disturbed and submissive species. - 2010 *

It's amazing how much insecurity we get rid of by focussing our attentions on others. - 2010 *

Would that I be remembered that in life I was a traveler and not a tourist. - 2007 *

To free ourselves from the spiritual and emotional shackles which bind us, we must know the difference between service and servitude. - 2007 *

*Se soumettre aux vouloirs des autres n'est pas générosité mais plutôt abdication - l'abandon d'une voix, d'une âme, d'une vie. - 2007 **

Crotchetiness does not make us worthy of the title elder anymore than being old makes us venerable. Sometimes, being old and miserable simply means we are old and miserable. - 2007 *

With so many of us searching for our inner child is it any wonder that a contemporary word for house is "crib"? - 2006 *

There is nothing weaker in the personality of an individual than that person's convictions framed in silence. - 2006 *

What is important is not what has been done to me but what I do with what has been done to me. . . 2006 *

I would rather be thought a cynical, sarcastic pessimist than a submissive fool. - 2006 *

We are so much the lesser when we consider the existence of others only in relation to our own. - 2003 *

May the world recognize our extraordinary uniqueness in equal measure to the awe with which we behold others - 2002 *

One does not find oneself by looking into the safety that is within but rather by flying into and dealing with the unknown of the self which can only be discovered from without. - 2001 *

What if we wake up one morning to the horrible discovery that the "sexy statement" we chose to wear that day is nothing more than something in which we hide. - 2000 *

That we argue vehemently over verbal superficialities such as "fisherman", versus "fisher", "craftsman" versus "craftsperson", is not so much a search for equity as it is a grab for power at a time when we should be concerned about how edible the fish is and whether there will be any fish at all for a damned fisherman to catch. . . and us to eat. - 2000 *

*I'm under construction, improvements forthcoming - (Marc Charron) - a "wondrously wonderful wonder" of a man - 1998 **

A controlling ego should never be mistaken for a strong one. - 1998 *

To choose to become a better human being is a process of faith, not of controlling precepts. - 1998 *

*Lorsqu'on est neutre, on n'est pas. - 1998 **

How disturbing it is to see painters, musicians and other entertainers advertise their failings, follies and addictions as if, without them, they would never have become the most wonderful and successful and grandiose personas they announce to the world that they are. - 1997 *

How does one describe a society which for decades has thrived on descriptions of depravity, shared-in rather than alleviated the cry of victims, complained of incessant problems and failed to consider solutions other than to increase their pill dosage?
What do we say about a realm which then found comfort in sadness, scorned those who are not similar and found beauty in anorexic photo-copies of true life?
What does one say about a world which revelled in its own victimhood rather than encouraged heroism, celebrated revenge rather than pardoned and defined creativity as that which shocks, spits or rales? In the end, what do we say about an environment which found solace in the lowest common denominator rather than stimulated growth and progress in the nourishment of souls? What can one say about the denying 70s, the numb 80s and the ever-more vicious and frightened 90s?"Vive le reality TV libre?"- 1997 *

I once saw an elderly woman crossing with difficulty a wide boulevard. From nowhere appeared a boy. He gently approached the frail woman struggling. She looked up. He smiled back and offered his arm. She took it and they slowly edged towards the curb. Seeing her safe, Sir Galahad crossed back from whence he came. But before he rushed off, as boys do, he looked to her and she to him - both smiling across that great divide. - 1997 *

A healthy ego is dependent on a combination of naïve optimisms, a desire to better the lives of others and a measured dose of denial of what is. - 1997 *

Yesterday's rebel is oftentimes today's cringing submissive. - 1997 *

It is not necessary to feel good in order to function. - 1995 *

Status is the goal of those who fail to achieve. - 1995 *

*Know thyself! A maxim as pernicious as it is ugly. Whoever observes himself arrests his own development. A caterpillar who wanted to know itself well would never become a butterfly. - (André Gide) author and Nobel laureate (1869-1951) *

It's horrible to no longer be five years old - when being cute was enough. - *

Far better it is to be an uneducated intelligent being than a qualified idiot. - *

Even children are smart enough to know that who they are is what they do. - *

Through subterfuge, Reality TV has taught us to focus on our inner loser – not on our innate capacity to strive and overcome. It has taught us to emote rather than think and to berate and belittle our and the needs of others to reach beyond being the best we can be. - *

Solitude is to enjoy the company of one's "self" - loneliness is to find no one there. - *

It is possible to draw and paint if you are afraid of the world but impossible if you are afraid of yourself. - *

Whether our recall needs to tarnish or varnish the past depends heavily on how we deal with the present and how we perceive the present to be dealing with us. - *

When we refuse to live other than within the confines of our emotional pain we assure ourselves a notoriously secure environment in which we will never be released from its grasp. - *

Ignorance does not create anxiety. The belief that we are a fool because we are ignorant does. *

In a quest to look younger, women are more astute than men. To shave off ten years, they get a face lift. Whereas, men put on a baseball cap - shaving ten points off their IQ. - *

Sameness. Nothing less than a bland soup who's ingredients can only be listed as a spoonful , a cup full, a quart full of nothing. - *

To radiate, a bulb must glow. - *

It rained. . . I cried for sun.
It was hot. . . I cried for breeze.
The wind whistled. . . I cried for calm.
Aging. . . I cried for youth.
Dying. . . the world breathed a sigh of relief. - *

Living to the age of 100 is not, in and of itself, an accomplishment. Better to die young and well thought of than to live so long we begin to weigh heavy on the souls of others. - *

If we perceive ourselves living life as paupers because of the professional choices we have made, then without question our lives will be impoverished. - *

Succeeding in life is not as easy or as wonderful as it sounds. Those who knew of us before "success" often ask why not me? And then there are those who know us not and can only say how "lucky" we are. Then there are those who love us and know very well how difficult the road has been, how passionately we have embraced the challenge and how much we needed to surpass even the best that we could be. And so we smile. - *

We often refer to ourselves as "who we are" as if we need convincing - as if we feel the pain of lack of recognition in our lives. Why is it we are so afraid of being recognized by "what we do"? Is it because we equate "doing" with lowly labour and "who we are" with some higher level of creativity or prestige? Or is it because we are afraid that everyone will discover that we don't really "do" anything? - *

We are all ultimately free of any and all restraints - except those we impose upon our "selves". - *

Bernard Aimé Poulin - Biography

Bernard Poulin works internationally as a painter of official, corporate and private portraits. His subjects range from prominent members of the world's political, royal, corporate, artistic, sport and religious elite to private family and child representations.

His clients have included the governments of Canada, Bermuda and Ontario as well as corporations, institutions and associations such as the Canadian Pacific Railway, the National Research Council of Canada, the Royal College of Physicians and Surgeons of Canada and the Royal Collections of both Windsor Castle and St-James Palace in London.

Since 1995 investing patrons have been commissioning private thematic exhibitions of Bernard Poulin's work, purchasing the collections sight unseen. These exhibitions have focused on Tuscany, Venice (1996), Provence, (1998), Jerusalem (2000), Paris (2004 & 2005) and a Grand Tour Exhibition in 2007.

The author also sculpts in bronze, using the lost wax process. As a muralist and sculptor he has created several three-dimensional projects using acrylic, bronze, black marble and maple. These can be found in the lobby of the Children's Hospital of Eastern Ontario, the Ottawa Children's Aid Society and the Solange Karsh Center for Medical Research.

A noted lecturer, Bernard Poulin has participated in the creation of a dozen books dedicated to the process of drawing and portraiture. His articles and television appearances have been translated into Portuguese and Italian. He is the author of 11 of his own books. His *"The Complete Colored Pencil Book"*, was published by FW Publications (North Light division) in1992. The first edition sold more than 75,000 copies. Its French translation, *(Le crayon de couleur),* was published in Paris in 1995. The soft-cover re-issue of the *Complete Colored Pencil Book* appeared in 2002 and was again re-released in a revised version under the banner of the Classics Series of North Light books in 2011. In December 2010 *"Beyond Discouragement - Creativity"* was published as an essay on the effects of the past century on creativity. In 2012, Bernard's *Please Daddy, Hold My Hand* (a tribute to the bond between fathers and sons) was published by Mirror Comics of Ottawa. In 2014, this same book was reformatted and published as a children's book entitled : "Hold My Hand".

In 2011 the Assemblée parlementaire de la francophonie internationale (the association of the world's French parliaments) conferred upon Bernard the title of Chevalier (Knight) of the *Ordre de la Pléiade* - in recognition of his international efforts in both the visual arts and the French fact.

Though a biography of the artist is published in both the *Canadian Who's Who* and *A Dictionary of Canadian Artists, a more complete biogrpahy is availanble on the artist's website.* Bernard Poulin is represented by agents in Paris France, Bermuda, Kelowna, Ottawa and Sudbury. *For more information please visit :*

Bernard Aimé Poulin - Biographie courte

Artiste-peintre et portraitiste international depuis 48 ans, Bernard Poulin cré des portraits officiels et privés de personnages variés don't plusieurs provenant de l'élite royale, politique, corporative et sportive du monde. Son oeuvre, recherché par les gouvernements du Canada, des Bermudes et de l'Ontario répond aussi à la demande d'organismes et de sociétés tels Le Canadien Pacifique, le Conseil national de recherche Canada, le Collège royal des chirurgiens et médecins ainsi que les Collections royales du Palais St-James et du Château Windsor au Royaume-Uni.

Depuis 1995, des mécènes-investisseurs se regroupent pour commander des expositions complètes - traitant de sujets tels : la Toscane et Venise (1996), Provence (1998), Jérusalem (2000), Paris (2004 & 2005) et une exposition grande tournée en 2007. Ces expositions sont payées avant même d'être créées.

Bernard Poulin est *aussi sculpteur (le bronze)* et muraliste. Il a réalisé plusieurs projets tridimensionnels, don't celui à l'entrée principale de *l'Hôpital des enfants de l'est de l'Ontario*, celui du *Centre de recherche médicale Solange Karsh* et celui (sculpture en bronze et marbre) dans le hall principal de la *Société de l'Aide à l'enfance à Ottawa*.

Depuis des décennies le peintre est conférencier et chef d'atelier au Canada, aux États-Unis et aux Bermudes. Il a participé à la réalisation de plusieurs livres de techniques du dessin et on a déjà traduit de ses articles en italien. En plus, 6 émissions télévisées de son enseignement, produites par TVO, ont été traduites en portugais.

Poulin est auteur de 11 livres, donc 5 sur le dessin. Sa création : *The Complete Colored Pencil Book*, a été publiée en 1992. Sa traduction, intitulée *Le crayon de couleur,* a été réalisée à Paris en 1995 par la maison *Ulysseditions*. Une réédition (en couverture souple) est entamée en 2002 et rééditée en 2011 dans la série classique de *North Light*. Books. En 2010 Bernard publie un essai sur la créativité intitulé : *Beyond Discouragement - Creativity*. En 2012, une reconnaissance des liens précieux entre pères et fils est publiée sou le titre: *Please Daddy, Hold My Hand*. Cette création, illustrée par Dominic Bercier, est réalisée sous forme de bande dessinée par Mirror Comics d'Ottawa et en 2014, sous forme de livre d'enfant.

En 1990 l'association *Hadassah WIZO du Canada* cré la *Bourse Bernard Aimé Poulin*. En mars 2011, L'Assemblée parlementaire de la francophonie (mondiale) lui confère le grade de Chevalier de l'Ordre de la Pléiade - reconnaissant ces efforts dans la promotion des arts visuels et de la francophonie mondiale.

Quoique la biographie du peintre est disponible chez le *Canadian Who's Who* et se retrouve au *A Dictionary of Canadian Artists,* un résumé plus complet est disponible sur le site web du peintre. Les agents de l'artiste se retrouvent à Paris, aux Bermudes, à Kelowna, à Ottawa et à Sudbury.
Pour plus de renseignements , svp vous adresser au *: www.bernardpoulin.com*

Other Books By The Author

2014	Hold My Hand (children's book)
2012	Please Daddy, Hold My Hand (comic book)
2011	The Complete Colored Pencil Book (Classic series)
2010	Beyond Discouragement-Creativity
1994	Le crayon de couleur (Paris)
1992 +	The Complete Colored Pencil Book (various editions)
1989	Creative Illustration - Colored pencil techniques - Bk 4
1989	Special Effects - Colored pencil techniques - Bk 3
1989	Blending Color - Colored pencil techniques - Bk 2
1989	Basic Skills - Colored pencil techniques - Bk 1
1980	MiG (a compendium of published cartoons)
1975	Io e Firenze (travelogue)